CHILD CARE CRISIS

A Reference Handbook

CHILD CARE CRISIS

A Reference Handbook

Diane Lindsey Reeves

CONTEMPORARY WORLD ISSUES

ABC-CLIO

Santa Barbara, California
Denver, Colorado
Oxford, England

Library of Congress Cataloging-in-Publication Data

Reeves, Diane Lindsey, 1959–
    Child care crisis : a reference handbook / Diane Lindsey Reeves.
      p. cm.—(Contemporary world issues)
    Includes bibliographical references and index.
    1. Child care services—United States. 2. Child care services—
Government policy—United States. I. Title. II. Series
    HQ778.7.U6R44 1992   362.7′12—dc20   92-38144

ISBN 0-87436-645-3 (alk. paper)

99 98 97 96 95 94 93 92   10 9 8 7 6 5 4 3 2 1

ABC-CLIO, Inc.
130 Cremona Drive, P.O. Box 1911
Santa Barbara, California 93116-1911

This book is printed on acid-free paper ∞.
Manufactured in the United States of America

Contents

6 Nonprint Resources, 87

7 State-by-State Child Care Profiles, 97

Preface

Overview of Child Care in the United States

Over the last few decades, dramatic social changes have brought about fundamental shifts in American demographics and family structure. The majority of American children now live in families with either two working parents or a single working parent. These parents face an ongoing challenge in finding good, quality, reliable, and affordable child care. At first glance, this may seem to be a wholly personal dilemma. In reality, however, it is also society's dilemma because an entire generation—and a nation's future—is at risk.

Government institutions—both federal and state—have been slow to recognize the growing child care crisis and even slower to act; businesses have not done much better. While policymakers, legislators, and corporate decision makers argue, debate, and all too often avoid dealing with child care issues, millions of parents and children struggle with the realities of a fragmented and often inadequate system of child care provision. Their struggles affect not only children's and families' well-being, but productivity and effectiveness in the workplace. In short, their problem is America's problem.

The Growing Need for Child Care

The traditional model for the American family includes a working father and a mother who stays home to care for the children. Modern society, however, provides and often makes necessary a number of additional options. Mothers who work outside the home are hardly a new phenomena — working class mothers have always held jobs in addition to the tasks of homemaking and raising children. Over the past three decades, however, they have been joined in the labor force by millions of middle-class women. This trend is partly the result of increased opportunities for women. But for many, if not most families, two incomes are necessary to maintain a median standard of living. Single and divorced parents face even more challenges.

By the year 2000, the United States labor force will include an estimated 66.8 million women—nearly 62 percent of all women over 16 and 80 percent of women of childbearing age. In fact, women with preschool-age children currently constitute the fastest growing group within the U.S. labor force. Many of these women are single parents—more than 11 million children currently live in families maintained by women.

Fathers are also affected by child care issues. More than a third of male workers have children under the age of 18. Two-thirds of these men have wives who are also in the labor force ; one million children live in homes maintained by single fathers. Increasingly, men are assuming more of the child care responsibilities in both one- and two-parent households.

Effects of Nonparental Child Care on Children and Parents

The effects of nonparental care on childhood development are uncertain and difficult to evaluate depending upon variables such as the quality of care, the age of the child, the home environment, and the child's personality. The results of studies are mixed. Concern is greatest for infants and very young children with some studies indicating that infants in day care have trouble forming secure attachments to their parents; other studies have found patterns of increased aggression, less cooperation, and higher frustration levels among children who experienced early nonparental care. Still other studies, however, have shown that children in day care have better social skills, demonstrate greater independence, and are more self-confident than those cared for by stay-at-home parents.

Guilt is a constant companion for many working parents. Problems associated with finding, keeping, and paying for child care often spill over into the workplace. Child care difficulties are a major cause of worker absenteeism, tardiness, and inability to concentrate, as well as higher stress levels and resultant health problems.

Society's Response to Child Care Needs

Until recently, child care has been an invisible issue. While low-income families have always struggled with the issue of child care, it has become more of a mainstream issue as the problem of obtaining and paying for quality child care has spread into other segments of society. A number of additional factors has contributed to it becoming a national issue. Among these are the following:

> Though they are still very much a minority in the halls of power, women hold an increasing number of local, state, and national offices. Family - and child-related issues are a top priority for many of these women who have worked hard to pass legislation and set "family-friendly" policies, including support for, and adequate regulation of, child care.

> Both male and female office holders have become more aware of the power of women voters. Media coverage has helped to sensitize policymakers to the issues women consider important, including child care.

> The tremendous influx of women into the labor force has forced employers to deal with problems of absenteeism, tardiness, and decreased productivity due to family-related problems, including difficulties with finding, keeping, and paying for child care.

Despite this increased awareness, progress has been slow. Although a greater quantity of legislation has been introduced, Congress has been reluctant to act on child care, and much of the legislation that did make it through the Senate and House died on the president's desk.

Likewise, most businesses have been slow to change their employee policies and practices to take into account changing family structures and needs. Some employers, particularly at the largest corporations, are beginning to move toward more family-friendly policies such as flexible hours, on-site child care centers, and family sick leave. While such enlightened companies are still very much in the minority, many more businesses have an increasing awareness of child care as an important factor in the workplace.

Child care workers face the additional problems of low status and low pay, ranking well beneath dog groomers and garbage collectors in occupational prestige and compensation. As a consequence, turnover is high, forcing child care professionals to leave the profession due to insufficient salaries, lack of respect, and burnout.

The Current Status of Child Care in America

Over a two year period, beginning in 1987, the National Research Council's Committee on Child Development Research and the Public Policy Panel on Child Care has conducted an in-depth study on the costs, effects, and feasibility of alternative child care policies and programs. The panel reached seven general conclusions about the status of child care:

1. Existing child care services in the United States are inadequate to meet current and anticipated future needs of children, parents, and society.
2. A large number of children are presently cared for in settings that do not protect their health and safety and do not provide appropriate developmental stimulation.
3. Families with infants and toddlers, those with children with disabilities, those with mildly or chronically ill children, those with school-age children, and those in which parents work nontraditional schedules often have particular difficulties arranging appropriate child care services.
4. Economically disadvantaged families are often precluded from quality child care situations because of financial and informational limitations.
5. Existing child care services are a diverse system of providers, programs, and institutions that have little interconnectedness and do not share a common purpose or direction.
6. No single policy or program can address the child care needs of families and children. A comprehensive array of coordinated policies and programs is needed that addresses the needs of families in different social, economic, and cultural circumstances as well as the needs of children of different ages, stages of development, and abilities.

7. While the centrality of parental rights and responsibilities
    in child rearing must be honored and preserved,
    responsibility for meeting the nation's child care needs
    should be shared by individuals, families, voluntary
    organizations, employers, communities, and government
    at all levels.

The Future of Child Care

Much attention and lip service is being paid to the needs of families
and children today, yet the reality is that those needs are not being
met. If we are to ensure that society's youngest members receive the
care and nurturing they need to grow into mature, healthy, and
productive citizens, many changes must be made soon. At a minimum these changes include:

Recognition of the needs of children as priorities—in word,
action, and spending. While the needs of parents, employers,
and society are crucial factors in formulating public policy
and programs, the well-being of children must be a foremost
consideration in every decision.

Acceptance of the fact that child care is not just a women's
issue, but a men's issue, a business issue, a government issue,
and a society issue.

Commitment to ensuring that adequate child care options are
available to every family that needs them. This includes
providing sufficient quality to ensure the best possible
developmental environment for children, along with
protection of each family's right to choose what's best for its
members, including both children and parents.

Consistent and fair regulatory policy and enforcement of
minimum quality standards for all types of child care
situations. of a national level!!!

Workplace policies that enable parents to balance their dual roles as productive worker and nurturing parent.

Tax structures that respect the diverse needs and make-up of modern families, including single-parent and two-working parent families as well as those families in which one parent remains at home to care for the children.

Adequate compensation systems and career growth ladders for child care providers.

This volume looks at child care as a multi-faceted, complex social issue, providing an overview of major developments in public policy surrounding child care. It also provides a look at the current patchwork system of child care and examines its costs and effects. In exploring what is and what has been, perhaps we can gain insight into what can be. It is from this framework that new ideas and innovations must spring. The future of an entire generation of children—and indeed, of our nation—depends upon providing every child with a healthy start in life—physically, mentally, emotionally, and socially. With the majority of our nation's children requiring some form of nonparental child care, the development of a comprehensive, inclusive, and high-quality child care system must be among our national priorities.

How To Use This Book

This book is meant to serve both as a one-stop resource and as a guide to further research. Chapter 1 is a chronology of significant social, political, judicial, and legislative developments related to child care since the establishment of the first day care center in Boston in 1828. Chapter 2 contains biographical sketches of key activists, experts, and policymakers. Chapter 3 includes factual and statistical information, including demographic information, a summary of child care options, the role of employers in child care, an examination of the costs of child care, indicators of quality child care, and an overview of current government policies and laws regarding child care. Chapter 4 is an annotated directory of public and private agencies and organizations, including research institutes and centers. Chapter 5 is an annotated bibliography of print resources, including books, reports, and periodicals. Chapter 6 is an annotated list of nonprint resources, including videos and databases. Also included is a glossary of important terms and acronyms.

References

Bureau of the Census. *Who's Minding the Kids?* Current Population Reports, Series P-70, No. 9. Washington, DC: U.S. Department of Commerce, 1987.

Bureau of Labor Statistics. *Marital and Family Characteristics of the Labor Force.* Washington, DC: U.S. Department of Labor, March 1988.

National Commission on Children. *Beyond Rhetoric: A New American Agenda for Children and Families.* Washington, DC: Government Printing Office.

1

Chronology

MANY OF THE CHILD CARE ISSUES prevalent 150 years ago have yet to be resolved in modern-day America: the two-tiered system of child care in which quality is often proportional to a family's ability to purchase it; conflict between the traditional role of mother in the home versus mother in the workplace; concerns about the role of child care in a child's early development; and demand/supply inequities. Also of note is the social stigma attached to government-sponsored child care programs, such as welfare relief programs and/or support for dysfunctional families.

There has also been an ongoing trend of "reactionary social policy" in which child care becomes a mainstream issue only in times of economic or national crisis. While war and economic depression forced governmental and business response to child care in the past, dramatic changes in work force and family demographics are the factors that have brought this issue to the forefront in our nation today.

The following chronological summary highlights the milestones of a nation's response to the societal and economic role of child care.

1828   First American day care center opened as Boston Infant School. The center was established to provide care for 18-month-old to 4-year-old children and to enable poor mothers to seek employment. The philosophy of the program was to form a religious and moral foundation in young disadvantaged children that would later enable them to escape poverty.

1854   First American "crèche" established at the Children's Hospital in New York City to provide extended (12–14 hours per day) daytime care and medical attention for children aged 13 weeks to 3 years. This center and many other programs established in the 1880s and 1890s catered to the needs of European immigrants and rural Americans looking for better opportunities in the industrial centers.

1898   The National Federation of Day Nurseries was founded in an attempt to promote high standards of care. At that time, 175 day nurseries were operating in the United States, though the need for care far exceeded the supply.

1909   President Theodore Roosevelt convened the first White House Conference on Children.

1911   The Mothers Pension Act was enacted in 40 states. This act called for support payments that would enable women to stay home and care for their own children. Pensions were generally limited to wives and children of deceased, incapacitated, insane, or imprisoned men. Women able to earn a good wage were excluded from eligibility.

1919   Day nurseries emphasizing parent education were opened in the public schools of Los Angeles, California, and Gary, Indiana.

The International Labor Organization's Maternity Protection Convention called for a paid maternity leave for at least 12 weeks (a minimum of 6 weeks before and after childbirth), job protection during maternity leave, full medical care or health insurance benefits, and nursing breaks during working hours. By 1951, 18 countries had ratified the convention. The United States has yet to ratify the convention.

1920   Experimental nursery school programs were set up for research in child care and development in cities in New York, Michigan, Massachusetts, Maryland, and California.

1933   Roosevelt's Federal Emergency Relief Act and Works Progress Administration (WPA) provided federal funds for day nurseries and nursery schools in a Depression-era effort to provide employment for preschool teachers and other personnel. Two-thirds of these programs were located in public schools. Although this was the government's first financial commitment to child care, the emphasis of the action was more on getting the unemployed off welfare than on benefiting children.

1935   Title V of the Social Security Act passed, allowing for grants-in-aid for child care services and research. Designated funds were administered through state departments of public welfare.

1937   Some 40,000 children were enrolled in approximately 1,500– 1,900 WPA-supported child care programs. Two-thirds of these programs were housed in public schools.

1938   WPA support for child care was discontinued.

1941   The Lanham Act (Public Law 137) allocated partial funding to set up child care centers in defense plants employing women. A total of $51,922,977 in federal funds and $26,008,839 in state funds was disbursed under the Lanham Act for the development of 3,102 centers serving approximately 600,000 children. Through this funding, 1,150 of the original WPA nurseries were supported. It is estimated that these centers served only 40 percent of child care needs at that time.

1943   Kaiser Industries Corporation opened the nation's first employer-sponsored child care center, serving a total of 4,019 children 24 hours a day.

1963   Congress allocated $800,000 to aid local child care programs and to develop new ones through the welfare system.

1964   Project Head Start, a large-scale government social reform effort to engage in compensatory education programs for environmentally and economically disadvantaged children, was launched and funded. The program emphasized parent education and involvement as well as early enrichment for pre-school-age children. A major goal of the program was to interrupt the cycle of poverty at an early age level. The program was originally part of the Economic Opportunity Act (Public Law 88452) and President Johnson's War on Poverty program.

1969   KinderCare established its first center in Montgomery, Alabama.

1970   The White House Conference on Children identified child care as one of the major problems facing the American family.

1971   President Richard Nixon vetoed the Comprehensive Child Development Act. The act had been designed to provide child care funds for welfare recipients, funds for the creation of additional child care services, sliding-scale funding for single parents and working families, and expansion of the Head Start program.

1971
cont.
The Tax Revision Bill was enacted, raising child care deductions from $900 to a maximum of $4,800 a year.

1972
The National Council of Jewish Women published *Windows on Day Care,* the results of a national survey of child care situations.

The Office of Child Development funded the development of a professional training program for child care workers, a course of study resulting in a child development associate degree.

1976
The Democratic presidential platform proposed "federally financed, family centered, developmental and educational child care programs . . . available to all who need and desire them."

1978
Federal Employees Flexible and Compressed Work Schedules Act allowed eligible employees of federal agencies to have flexibility in arranging work schedules.

The Pregnancy Discrimination Act stated that women affected by pregnancy, childbirth, or other related medical conditions are to be granted the same consideration as other workers with disabilities.

Abt Associates published the findings of a four-year study of center-based child care in the United States. Findings revolved around three key policy variables, now referred to as the "iron triangle"— group size, caregiver:child ratio, and caregiver qualifications.

1979
The United Nations proclaimed the International Year of the Child to mark the twentieth anniversary of the U.N. Declaration of the Rights of the Child.

1980
The Federal Interagency Day Care Requirements set minimum quality standards regarding adult:child ratio, classroom group size, and child-related training of staff for federally sponsored programs. Implementation of the standards was permanently suspended by Public Law 9735 in 1981.

The *Dictionary of Occupational Titles,* a U.S. Department of Labor publication, classified child care workers in the same skill category as restroom attendants, porters, and dog groomers.

1981   Title XX funding was transformed into Social Service Block Grants administered to states for various social services, including child care. The funds were designated to be used at the discretion of individual states.

1983   The IRS added a line to the short income tax form (1040A) that allowed parents to claim the child care tax credit. In previous years this credit had been available only to users of the long form 1040.

1984   The High/Scope Educational Research Foundation released a report, based on a 22-year study, on the impact high-quality preschool experiences can have on the lives of disadvantaged children. The report, *The Effects of the Perry Preschool Program on Youths Through Age 19,* concluded that participation in quality preschool programs "made a significant difference in the lives of disadvantaged children and led to clear-cut economic savings for states and local communities" in terms of remedial efforts.

1985   A report issued by the Child Advocacy Office of the National Council of Churches of Christ concluded that churches and synagogues (through their own church-run programs or through renting church facilities to outside groups) formed the largest group of day care providers in the United States, estimating that "for every child who enters the church on Sunday for church school, eight enter on Monday for a weekday child care program."

1986   Funding for child care programs was decreased in 29 states.

1987   A U.S. Census Bureau report estimated that the annual total cost of child care for working parents was $11 billion.

1988   More than 100 child care-related bills were introduced in Congress. Of these, the Act for Better Child Care Services (also known as the ABC Bill; S. 1885) was the first major child care bill introduced in Congress since Nixon vetoed the Child Care Development Act in 1971.

PBS broadcast the hour-long documentary "Who Cares for the Children? The State of Child Care in America" during the Week of the Young Child.

1988
cont.
Phyllis Schlafly led a "Baby Buggy Brigade" to Washington, D.C., in protest of the ABC Bill, claiming that it discriminated against mothers who were not in the work force.

Reports on growth within the child care industry cited the following groups as the largest providers of child care services: Department of Defense (638 centers), KinderCare (1,135 centers), La Petite Academy (600 centers), and Gerber Children's Centers (127 centers).

1989
Results from the Child Care Employee Project study of 227 centers were released. Significant among the findings was the impact of low wages and lack of benefits on the quality of care and turnover of staff.

Wellesley College's School-Age Child Care Project determined that approximately 17 percent of the nation's school districts offered some form of before- and after-school care or allowed community groups to sponsor programs in school facilities.

1990
A U.S. Census report estimated that 9.1 million children under the age of 5 were in some type of child care situation.

Congress allotted a $2.5 billion Child Care and Development Grant. The Block Grant designates 75 percent of its funds in assistance to the "working poor" and 25 percent for use in improving quality in all types of child care programs.

Representatives from more than 70 countries participated in the U.N. World Summit for Children.

President Bush vetoed the Family and Medical Leave Act, which required employers to grant up to three months of protected unpaid leave to employees who need to care for a newborn, an adopted child, an ill child, or another ill family member. The veto left the United States and South Africa as the only industrialized nations that have no family leave legislation.

IBM established a $22 million Child Care Resources Fund to be used to develop and enhance child care services in locales with a high concentration of IBM employees.

1991
Among the recommendations made in a comprehensive report issued by the National Commission on Children were "that government and all private sector employers establish family oriented policies and practices—including family and medical leave policies

1991
cont.
and flexible work scheduling alternatives and career sequencing—to enable employed mothers and fathers to meet their work and family responsibilities" and "that government at all levels, communities, and employers continue to improve the availability, affordability, and quality of child care services for all children and families that need them."

During the first session of the 102d Congress, the U.S. Senate voted 65 to 32 in favor of a family leave bill that would guarantee 12 weeks annually of protected leave to care for ailing parents or new children to employees of businesses with more than 50 employees. While the outlook for House approval looks promising, President Bush vetoed the current draft of the proposed bill.

References

Auerbach, Judith D. *In the Business of Child Care.* New York: Praeger, 1988.

Hymes, James L., Jr. *Early Childhood Education Twenty Years in Review: A Look at 1971–1990.* Washington, DC: National Association for the Education of Young Children, 1991.

National Commission on Children. *Beyond Rhetoric: A New American Agenda for Children and Families.* Washington, DC: 1991.

Steinfels, Margaret O'Brian. *Who's Minding the Children? The History and Politics of Day Care in America.* New York: Simon & Schuster, 1973.

Zigler, Edward F., and Mary E. Lang. *Child Care Choices.* New York: Macmillan, 1991.

2

Biographical Sketches

THIS CHAPTER PRESENTS BIOGRAPHICAL SKETCHES of some of the men and women who have made significant contributions to the field of child care. Representing a cross section of disciplines and at times widely divergent viewpoints, they all share a common interest in developing a child care system that meets the developmental needs of children and families and supports economic growth for businesses and communities. While there are countless others who could have been included in this chapter, those cited here were chosen because of the their long-standing career commitments to children and the national impact of their roles within the child care infrastructure. American children are fortunate to have on their side such tireless advocates as those featured in this chapter.

Jay Belsky

Jay Belsky is professor of human development at Pennsylvania State University. He received his Ph.D. in human development and family studies from Cornell University in 1978. Dr. Belsky, a recipient of a National Institute of Mental Health Research Scientist Development Award, has focused his research on a longitudinal study of families rearing and bearing their first children. An important aspect of this study has been addressing the influence of extensive nonparental care on infant and child development.

Dr. Belsky's current studies involve tracking developmental patterns from birth through a child's second-grade school year. All of his projects are concerned with the extent to which extensive nonparental care in the first year of life shapes subsequent experiences and development. The work is guided by the premise that routine day care as currently available in the United States is associated with attachment insecurity in infancy and aggression and noncompliance in the preschool and early elementary school years when it coincides with other contextual risks such as marital and/or economic distress.

Dr. Belsky has published more than 100 articles and chapters on related topics. He is the author of *Infancy, Childhood, and Adolescence* (1991) and *The Child in the Family* (1984) and editor of *Clinical Implications of Attachment* (1988).

Helen Blank

Helen Blank, as senior child care associate at the Children's Defense Fund, works to expand support for child care/early childhood development programs. Since 1982, she has authored six studies on state child care policies, as well as coauthored *The Child Care Handbook, Give More Children a Head Start,* and numerous articles and papers on child care policies.

As director of the Children's Defense Fund child care advocacy network, Ms. Blank developed *CDF Reports* and Child Watch, a project in collaboration with the Association of Junior Leagues that monitored the effects of the 1981 budget cutbacks on children and families.

Ms. Blank is a member of the Board of the Child Care Action Campaign, the Child Care Food Program Umbrella Sponsor's Steering Committee, the Advisory Board for the Child Care Employee Project, the National Center for Children in Poverty, and the Advisory Board of the National Council of the Jewish Women's Center for the Child.

T. Berry Brazelton

Based at the Harvard Medical School Department of Pediatrics, Dr. T. Berry Brazelton is the developer of the highly regarded Brazelton Neonatal Assessment Scale. His extensive research has centered on the parent-child relationship, new attitudes toward the development of gender identification, and the stresses and concerns of working parents. Quite often, his work has broadened to include a cross-cultural perspective; for instance, he conducted a comparative study of infant attachment and child-rearing practices in Kenya, Guatemala, Mexico, and Greece. He has also served as a consultant for the Chinese government concerning the one-child family and the training of pediatricians.

Dr. Brazelton is particularly known for his ability to translate scholarly research findings into highly readable lay terms. He is the author of several best-selling books on children, including *On Becoming a Family*, *Work and Caring*, and *Families: Crisis and Caring*. He also hosts the Lifetime cable television show *"What Every Baby Knows"* and authors a regular column in *Redbook* magazine.

In addition, Dr. Brazelton is the founder of Parent Action, a grass-roots advocacy group dedicated to empowering parents to speak out for what they need so that they can do a good job raising their children. As a member of the president's National Commission for Children, he spent two years traveling around the country to assess the status of America's children and families. His findings and recommendations are included in the commission's report, *Beyond Rhetoric: A New American Agenda for Children and Families*.

Marian Wright Edelman

Founder and president of the Children's Defense Fund, Marian Wright Edelman has devoted her life to living out a message her parents instilled in her while she was growing up in the segregated Deep South, a message that she, as a young black girl, "could do and be anything, that race and gender are shadows, and that character, self-discipline, determination, attitude and service are the substance of life." Her work at the Children's Defense Fund is guided by her goal to make it "un-American for any child to be poor or to be left behind."

Ms. Edelman, a respected leader in the children's advocacy movement, is known as one of the nation's most ardent spokespersons on behalf of the American child. She has been granted more than 60 honorary degrees from institutions of higher learning around the country, as well as an impressive list of awards and other honors.

She is a member of the National Commission on Children and serves on the boards of the Center on Budget and Policy Priorities, Citizens for Constitutional Concerns, the Council on Foreign Relations, the March of Dimes, the NAACP Legal Defense and Educational Fund, and the National Alliance of Business.

David Elkind

David Elkind is a professor of child study at Tufts University in Medford, Massachusetts. He was formerly professor of psychology, psychiatry, and education at the University of Rochester. After receiving his doctorate at the University of California, Los Angeles, he was a

National Science Foundation senior postdoctoral fellow at Piaget's Institut d'Epistemologie Genetique in Geneva. His research has been in the areas of perceptual, cognitive, and social development, where he has attempted to build upon the research and theory of Jean Piaget.

Although Dr. Elkind's list of publications now numbers well over 400 items, including research papers, theoretical articles, book chapters, and 13 books, he is best known for three of his most recent books, *The Hurried Child, All Grown Up and No Place To Go,* and *Miseducation.* His works in progress include *Grandparenting: Understanding Today's Children* and a manual for parents titled *Parent Stress.*

A member of many professional organizations, Elkind also serves as a consultant to state education departments, clinics, and mental health centers as well as to government agencies and private foundations. He lectures extensively in the United States, Canada, and abroad. He is past president of the National Association for the Education of Young Children.

Dana E. Friedman

Dana E. Friedman is the cofounder and copresident of the Families and Work Institute, a national nonprofit organization that conducts research on business, government, and community efforts to help people balance their work and family lives. She designs national research studies, employee needs assessments, human resource strategic plans, and management training programs.

Dr. Friedman was previously a senior research associate at The Conference Board, a nonprofit business think tank, where she created the Work and Family Information Center in 1983. Prior to that, she worked at the Carnegie Corporation of New York, where she conducted a national study of corporate views on family issues that led to the development of the board's Information Center. She also spent six years in Washington, D.C., where she was a lobbyist for the Day Care Council of America and the Coalition for Children and Youth.

Friedman has published widely in many professional journals, and she writes a monthly column, "The Juggling Act," for *Working Woman* magazine.

She received her B.S. in child development from Cornell University, a master's degree in early childhood education from the University of Maryland, and a doctorate in social policy from Harvard University.

Ellen Galinsky

Ellen Galinsky is the copresident of the newly founded Families and Work Institute, a nonprofit institute that serves as a national clearinghouse on work and family life and conducts research on business, government, and community efforts to help employees balance their job and family responsibilities.

Previously, Galinsky was on the faculty of Bank Street College of Education, where she helped to institute study in the field of work and family life and directed numerous research projects concerned with work and family life, stress, and productivity.

Galinsky has published widely in academic journals and magazines, and her books include *The New Extended Family: Day Care That Works* (1977) and *The Six Stages of Parenthood* (1987). Her most recent book, *The Preschool Years* (1988), coauthored with Judy David, was selected as an alternate selection for the Book-of-the-Month Club and the Quality Paperback Book Club. She is executive editor of the newsletter *"Work and Family Life."*

Galinsky received her B.A. from Vassar College and her M.S. from Bank Street College. In November 1988, she was selected as one of the 100 outstanding women in America by *Ladies' Home Journal.*

Elinor Guggenheimer

Founder and first president of the Child Care Action Campaign, Elinor Guggenheimer has spent the last 40 years as an advocate for better child care. In the 1940s, Mrs. Guggenheimer founded the Day Care Council of New York. She has also chaired or served on Manhattan's Advisory Committee on Day Care, the Day Care and Child Development Council of America, the Mayor's Task Force on Child Development, the New York State Advisory Committee on Day Care, the City-Wide Parents' Association, the Committee for Community Control of Day Care, the New York State Joint Legislative Committee on Child Welfare, the National Association for the Education of Young Children, the Organization Mondiale Education Prescolare, the Child Welfare Legal American Activities, and the Governor's Commission on Child Care.

Guggenheimer has contributed a lifetime of public service. Among her many positions, she served as the commissioner of the New York City Department of Consumer Affairs between 1973 and 1978, and as a member of the New York City Planning Commission between 1961 and 1968. She has taught at the New School for Social

Research, York College of the City University of New York, and the Columbia University Teachers College, New York City Department.

In addition to serving as Child Care Action Campaign (CCAC) president, Guggenheimer is currently a member of the Disciplinary Committee of the Appellate Division of New York State Courts, a lifetime board member of the Community Service Society and the International Women's Forum, and honorary chair of the Council of Senior Centers and Services.

James L. Hymes, Jr.

For the last 20 years, Dr. James L. Hymes, Jr., has summarized highlights of each year's events relating to children in volumes published as *Early Childhood Education: The Year in Review.* He has served as president of the National Association for the Education of Young Children, as vice president of the Association for Childhood Education International, and as a member of the National Planning Committee for Head Start. During World War II he was in charge of two Kaiser Child Service Centers in Portland, Oregon.

Hymes has been professor of education specializing in early childhood education at the State University of New York at New Paltz, at George Peabody College for Teachers, and at the University of Maryland. A graduate of Harvard University, he earned his M.A. and Ed.D. degrees in child development and parent education at Teachers College, Columbia University. He now lives in California and is a lecturer and consultant in early childhood education.

Lillian Katz

Lillian Katz is professor of early childhood education and director of the ERIC Clearinghouse on Elementary and Early Childhood Education at the University of Illinois, Urbana-Champaign. She serves as editor-in-chief of *Early Childhood Research Quarterly* and as vice president of the National Association for the Education of Young Children. Her monthly column, "Three and Four Year Olds—As They Grow" appears in *Parents Magazine.*

Dr. Katz began her career in early childhood as a full-time mother of three and through her involvement in the San Francisco Bay Area Parent Cooperative Nursery Schools. She earned a B.A. from San Francisco State College and a Ph.D. in psychological studies from Stanford University.

She has a special interest in the implications of early childhood education in a cross-cultural setting and has participated as a visiting professor at universities in England, Australia, West Germany, India, the West Indies, China, and Canada.

Kathy Modigliani

As director of Wheelock College's Family Child Care Project, Modigliani works in the area of policy-relevant research and demonstration in the field of family child care. Her current activities include a study of the economics of family child care and the evaluation of community projects that support the quality of care through training, accreditation, and parent education. Formerly a research scientist and project director for the Bank Street College, Modigliani is a respected authority on many aspects of the child care profession. She is a frequent contributor to anthologies and monographs on issues related to child care, is a co-author of *Opening Your Door to Children: How To Start a Family Day Care Program* (Washington DC: National Association for the Education of Young Children), and is finishing work on her doctoral dissertation "Child Care as an Occupation: The Toughest Job You'll Ever Love" (Boston: Wheelock College).

Gwen Morgan

Gwen Morgan is a respected authority on child care administration, regulation, and policy. She has served as a board member of the National Association for the Education of Young Children and is a founding member of the Child Care Action Campaign. Formerly senior child care planner for the state of Massachusetts, Morgan is the author of more than 100 publications, including *The National State of Child Care Regulations.*

Morgan's extensive work in the child care field currently centers on three separate entities. As a founder of Work/Family Directions, Morgan has worked in such areas as planning national resource and referral services, working with state governments in developing partnership policies, compiling and publishing current data on state licensing policies, developing community studies for corporations, presenting child care policy reports to corporations, and developing publications, training, and management programs. She also works in quality enhancement for the Work/Family Directions Development Corporation in assessing community needs and business strategies, child care startup, and training. In addition, since 1989, Morgan has been project director of the Center for Child Care Training and Policy at Wheelock College.

Morgan has also participated in many national policy studies of child care, as either consultant or adviser. Projects of note include the National Day Care Supply Study, with the National Urban Institute and the National Association for the Education of Young Children; the National Child Care Salary and Staffing Study, with the National Child Care Employees Project; and the national studies conducted by Abt Associates on consumers of child care, child care centers, and home child care. Morgan was also involved in researching the legal aspects of federal regulation and the appropriateness study of the Federal Interagency Day Care Requirements established by the U.S. Department of Health, Education and Welfare.

Carol Brunson Phillips

Carol Brunson Phillips is executive director of the Council for Early Childhood Professional Recognition, Child Development Associate National Credentialing Program in Washington, D.C. She received her B.A. degree in psychology from the University of Wisconsin, her master's degree in early childhood education from Erikson Institute, and her Ph.D. in education from Claremont Graduate School. As a member of the human development faculty at Pacific Oaks College in Pasadena, California, she specialized in early childhood education and cultural influences on development for 13 years.

Patricia Scott Schroeder

U.S. Congresswoman Patricia Scott Schroeder (D-Colorado) is chair of the Select Committee on Children, Youth, and Families and is known for her efforts on behalf of women and children. She is the leading sponsor in the U.S. House of Representatives of the Family and Medical Leave Act, which gives workers a right to a job-guaranteed unpaid leave for family emergencies such as the birth, adoption, or serious illness of a child.

In an effort to put family issues on the national political agenda, Rep. Schroeder embarked in February 1988 on the Great American Family Tour, along with Harvard pediatrician Dr. T. Berry Brazelton, "Family Ties" television producer Gary David Goldberg, and director of the Institute for the Study of Women and Men at UCLA, Dr. Diana Meehan. Schroeder's work on family issues and her ideas for a twenty-first-century family policy agenda are outlined in her book *Champion of the Great American Family.*

Jules Sugarman

As national director of the Head Start program during its first five years, Jules Sugarman was instrumental in structuring and launching the successful preschool program. His distinguished career has also included serving as associate chief of the U.S. Children's Bureau, as vice chairman of the U.S. Civil Service Commission, and as a senior budget officer in three federal agencies. At the state and local levels, he has been secretary of Social and Health Services for the state of Washington, administrator of human resources for New York City, and chief administrative officer for the city of Atlanta. In the voluntary sector, he has served as executive director of Special Olympics International.

Sugarman has recently established the Center on Effective Services for Children, a not-for-profit organization dedicated to improving the effectiveness and efficiency of children's services.

Nancy Travis

Nancy Travis has been involved in every major development within the early childhood field in the past 50 years. She has worked in day care centers, nursery schools, day nurseries, "mother's day out" programs, parent cooperatives, gifted programs, Head Start programs, emergency care facilities, and family day care networks. She has licensed child care programs, provided training and technical assistance for such programs, developed dozens of professional publications, organized national child care conferences, and set up a metropolitan child care information and referral network. In fulfillment of a childhood dream, she helped set up child care programs in Nepal, Sri Lanka, Greece, Lebanon, and Brazil.

Director of Save the Children's Child Care Support Center in Atlanta since 1979, Travis works with both rural and urban communities, offering assistance in developing and implementing programs to help improve the quality of child care. She serves on a number of child care–related boards and committees. Of special note is her work with the Advisory Committee for the Alliance for Better Child Care, the National Resource Center for Children in Poverty, the Child Care Law Project, and the National Council of Jewish Women's Family Day Care Project.

Burton White

Dr. Burton White is founder and director of the Center for Parent Education, a nonprofit public service organization established in 1978. The center is devoted to educating parents and professionals about the importance of the first three years of life in relation to lifelong development. White is a strong advocate of supporting families in their role as the child's first educational delivery system and was instrumental in piloting the Missouri Parents as Teachers program from 1981 to 1985.

White's research has led him to the following recommendations concerning nonparental care for infants: (a) there should be no out-of-home care for children less than 6 months of age; (b) one person should care for the child in the child's home (preferably a grandparent or other relative with a strong attachment to the child) or, lacking that arrangement, care should be provided by, in the following order of suitability, one person caring for one child in a home other than that of the child; one person caring for three or four children in a family child care situation; a child care center with a low adult:child ratio.

Prior to his work at the Center for Parent Education, White was project director of the Harvard Preschool Project. His book *The First Three Years of Life* was nominated for the Pulitzer Prize in 1975.

Edward Frank Zigler

Edward Frank Zigler is Sterling Professor of Psychology and director of the Bush Center in Child Development and Social Policy at Yale University. It is in this role that he developed a child care/family support program called the School of the 21st Century, in which schools would become the hub of local child care services. This new branch of the educational system is designed to offer before- and after-school and vacation care to school-age children and all-day care to preschoolers. For children from birth to age 3, there is to be a family support and parent education program available to all families in the district. The program calls for a network of family day care providers to be trained and monitored by child care personnel in the schools, and a resource and referral system to assist parents with choosing child care and obtaining other social services. To date, 21st Century schools exist in Connecticut, Colorado, Missouri, Nebraska, Ohio, Texas, Wisconsin, and Wyoming.

Dr. Zigler served as the first director of the Office of Child Development and as chief of the Children's Bureau in 1971–1972. He was an architect of the Head Start program and of succeeding efforts, such as Project Follow Through, Home Start, the Child and Family Resource Program, and the Child Development Associate Program.

He has received many honors, including the "As They Grow" award in education from *Parents Magazine* in 1990, the Blanche F. Ittleson Memorial Lecture Award from the American Orthopsychiatric Association in 1989, and the Award for Distinguished Contributions to Psychology in the Public Interest from the American Psychological Association in 1982.

He is an author of *Child Care Choices: Balancing the Needs of Children, Families, and Society* (1991) and *The Parental Leave Crisis: Toward a National Policy* (with Meryl Frank; 1987), and coeditor, with Edmund W. Gordon, of *Day Care: Scientific and Social Policy Issues* (1982).

3

Facts and Data

AT FIRST GLANCE, THE ISSUE OF CHILD CARE may appear deceptively simple—someone watching someone else's children while the parents work. However, the picture becomes quite complex when you broaden the view to include the millions of American families using nonparental child care and add in the variables of different types of child care, multiple work schedules, changing developmental needs of children, and varying needs of employers, parents, and child care providers.

In recent years, studies on the multifaceted nature of child care have increased. Researchers are investigating the impact of nonparental child care on children. They have examined its effects on family dynamics and workplace productivity. They continue to look for systems that allow working parents to succeed at raising and supporting their families, which also enables businesses to thrive and prosper.

This chapter touches on each of these major issues and provides a synopsis of emerging trends concerning the diverse aspects of child care. It also summarizes recent legislative and government policy developments regarding child care.

ₗColorado Congresswoman Patricia Schroeder, "Government₋ ₁ics tell us that only one woman in 10 will get through life with the option to decide whether she wants to work. The other nine will have to work." Over the last four decades, the number of women in the work force has grown tremendously, particularly the number of married women with young children. According to unpublished data compiled by the U.S. Bureau of Labor Statistics, there has been a steady increase in the number of women (ages 16 and over) in the work force since the 1960s, as evidenced by the following statistics:

Year	Women in Population	Women in Labor Force	Percentage of Population
1960	61,582	23,240	37.7
1965	66,731	26,200	39.3
1970	72,782	31,543	43.3
1975	80,860	37,475	46.3
1980	88,348	45,487	51.5
1985	93,736	51,050	54.5
1990	98,399	56,554	57.5

Note: Numbers in thousands.
Source: U.S. Bureau of Labor Statistics, *Employment and Earnings* (January 1991, Table 2). Table prepared by Women's Bureau, DSEA, April 1991.

This dramatic surge of women into the labor force has created several changes in the traditional life pattern of the American female. Several trends are expected to continue into the next century. These include the following:

By 2000, it is expected that 66.8 million women will work outside the home, accounting for 47 percent of the labor force. This represents nearly 62 percent of all women of working age (16 years and over) and 80 percent of the women of childbearing age.

Women with infants make up the fastest-growing group in the labor force. As of 1988, 51 percent of all new mothers were working or looking for work before their baby's first birthday, 60 percent more than in the previous decade.

By 1995, experts estimate that two out of three preschoolers and four out of five school-age children will have mothers in the work force.

Nearly two-thirds of all mothers in the work force are single, widowed, divorced, separated, or have husbands who earn less than $15,000 a year.

Women are maintaining an increasing proportion of all families (16.9 percent in 1989). Nearly two-fifths (39 percent) of the 14 million increase in family households between 1969 and 1989 was attributable to families maintained by women. A total of 11.4 million children under age 18 live in families maintained by women. Of the 4 million children under age 6 living in single-parent households, 3.3 million live with single mothers.

Fathers

Child care is not just a women's issue. According to a fact sheet compiled by the U.S. House of Representatives Select Committee on Children, Youth, and Families, the role of working fathers concerning child care has also been affected by the changes of recent years:

In March 1990, 24.4 million fathers—36 percent of all males in the labor force—had children under the age of 18. Two-thirds of them had wives in the labor force. Some 12 million working fathers had children under the age of 6. Just over 1 million children were maintained by single fathers.

In 1987, fathers served as primary child care providers for 15 percent of children whose mothers worked part-time and for 7 percent of children whose mothers worked full-time.

A survey of 400 men and women with children under age 12 conducted for *Fortune* magazine by Bank Street College found that fathers were almost as likely as mothers to report that their jobs interfered with family life (37 percent versus 41 percent). A total of 30 percent of the fathers surveyed said that they had refused new jobs, promotions, or transfers because the changes would have meant less time with their families.

Child Care Options

Choosing an appropriate child care situation is a matter of parental right and responsibility. It involves the consideration of a number of factors, including the age(s) of the child(ren) needing care, working hours, home and work locations, family values, and education philosophy preferences. Following are descriptions of the most commonly used types of child care situations.

Nonparental Child Care

Family Child Care: A provider who takes care of children in her own home (family child care providers are almost always women). Providers of family child care are generally low- and moderate-income women representing a wide variety of skill and training backgrounds. As small business owners, these providers are responsible for the administrative tasks associated with running a business as well as for direct care of children.

Group Child Care Homes: A family child care provider who cares for a specified number of children in her home with assistance. Additional adults are employed as indicated by state requirements for staff:child ratios for the particular ages of the children receiving care.

Child Care Center: Care is provided in a program offered in a nonresidential facility that cares for more than 12 children. Types of center programs include full-day or part-day nursery schools, Head Start programs, and preschool.

In-Home Care: A person who provides care in the child(ren)'s own home. This type of care arrangement often involves a nanny or au pair. This is an expensive solution for full-time care, because one family pays the caregiver's entire salary. Also, the parents have the same tax obligations as any other employer.

Shared Care: This is an option in which two or more families employ someone to care for all of their children in one of the families' homes.

School-Age Child Care: This is care provided for children between the ages of 5 and 13 before and after school and during school vacations and holidays. School-age child care may be based in child care centers, family child care homes, churches/synagogues, public/private school facilities, or community recreation programs.

Parental Child Care

Within-Family Care: Some 47.8 percent of all working parents with children under age five arrange for child care within the family. This type of care includes arranging work hours so that one parent is always home; relying on relatives, older siblings, or close friends; or various combinations of these arrangements.

Distribution of Child Care Choices

According to a new study released by the U.S. Department of Education, in 1990 there were approximately 80,000 center-based early education and care programs with the capacity to care for over five million children in the United States. There was also approximately 118,000 regulated family child care providers with the potential to care for 860,000.

This report, *A Profile of Child Care Settings: Early Education and Care in 1990,* also cites the following trends:

The number of center-based child care programs has almost tripled since 1976–1977.

Across the country, center-based care tends to be scarcer in nonmetropolitan areas than in metropolitan areas, while regulated family child care is equally available in nonmetropolitan and metropolitan areas.

Vacancies in both center-based and family child care programs are concentrated in fewer than half of all programs.

There is an acute lack of center-based care of infants and toddlers with fewer than 10 percent of all vacancies available for this age group.

The following table provides an overview of key characteristics of the major types of center-based and family child care situations.

PROFILES OF EARLY EDUCATION AND CARE SETTINGS, 1990

| | Nonprofit Centers | | | | For-Profit Centers | | Regulated Family Child Care Programs |
	Head Start	Public Schools	Religious-Sponsored	Other Sponsor	Independent	Chain	Independent	
Average Total Enrollment	50	58	73	58	63	91	67	6
Average Percentage of Children Enrolled Who Are Age 3 to 5	99%	83%	74%	74%	69%	48%	59%	39%
Average Percentage of Children Enrolled Who Are Members of Minority Groups	57%	48%	22%	45%	27%	21%	21%	19%
Average Percentage of Children Enrolled Who Are From Families Receiving Public Assistance	68%	n.a.	5%	30%	10%	6%	8%	5%
Average Percentage of Teachers Who Have a College Degree	45%	88%	50%	52%	49%	31%	35%	11%
Average Hourly Wage of Teachers	$9.67	$14.40	$8.10	$8.46	$7.40	$5.43	$6.30	$4.04
Average Annual Teacher Turnover Rate	20%	14%	23%	25%	25%	39%	27%	n.a.
Average Hourly Fee Charged by Programs that Charge Fees	a	$1.19	$1.65	$1.39	$1.73	$1.47	$1.53	$1.64
Sample Size	231	255	240	131	402	94	459	583

Note: n.a. means not available
a Small sample size.
Source: Profile of Child Care Settings Study (Mathematica Policy Research, Inc., 1990).

According to the U.S. Bureau of the Census report *Who's Minding the Children,* in the fall of 1987 children under five years of age were cared for in the following ways:

Care in child's home, 29.9 percent

    By mother, 15.3 percent

    By other relative, 8.4 percent

    By nonrelative, 6.2 percent

Care in another home, 35.6 percent

    By relative, 13.3 percent

    By nonrelative, 22.3 percent

Child care center/preschool, 24.4 percent

Child cares for self, 0.3 percent

Mother cares for child at work, 8.9 percent

Other arrangements, 1.0 percent

Latchkey Children

Estimates of the number of school-age children (between 5 and 13 years old) who care for themselves before and/or after school range from 2 million (U.S. Census Bureau) to 15 million (Children's Defense Fund). Surveys in local communities indicate that as many as 25 percent of school-age children are on their own after school.

According to social scientist Ed Zigler, latchkey children represent more than 50 percent of the child care problem, and they are the easiest part of the problem to solve. In his book *Child Care Choices,* Zigler explains that "people have got to realize that there is a connection between leaving children unsupervised after school and such social problems as teenage pregnancy, juvenile delinquency and the use of drugs." In his innovative School for the 21st Century blueprint, Zigler recommends using public school facilities—already paid for by taxpaying parents—for child care services.

Effects of Nonparental Child Care

Effects on Children

In a study commissioned by *Fortune* magazine, researchers from Bank Street College interviewed 405 employed parents, ranging from professionals and executives to manual and service workers, about the effects they felt child care had on their children.

Disadvantages

In order of concern, the respondents felt that their children suffered the following disadvantages stemming from participation in child care:

1. Rushed to conform to parents' schedule
2. Not given enough time or attention
3. Too susceptible to peer pressure
4. Don't always feel safe being alone
5. Overindulged because parents feel guilty
6. Spend too much time alone
7. Don't feel cared about enough
8. Spend too much time with other children

Advantages

Respondents also felt that their children benefited from child care in the following ways (in order of concern):

1. Are more independent
2. Are more socially adept from being with children
3. Are more self-confident
4. Have interesting role models for parents
5. Understand about the world of work
6. Learn more from child care

Effects on Infants and Toddlers

More controversy exists over the effects of nonparental care on very young children. Among those who believe that infants and toddlers should not be placed in substitute child care situations are Penelope

Leach, author of the influential child-raising book *Your Baby and Child;* Burton White, author of *A Parent's Guide to the First Three Years;* and child psychologist Jay Belsky. According to Belsky, two trends are beginning to surface in research:

1. Infants in day care are more likely to develop insecure attachments to their parents.
2. Follow-up studies of children with a record of early nonparental care show more serious aggression, less cooperation, less tolerance of frustration, more misbehavior, and at times social withdrawal.

While the complex interaction of many factors makes it difficult to make across-the-board judgments, researchers from the National Center for Clinical Infant Programs have agreed that "when parents have access to stable child care arrangements featuring skilled, sensitive and motivated caregivers, there is every reason to believe that both children and families can thrive."

In addition to the quality of the program, factors such as a child's temperament, family status, and economic background affect how well he or she adapts to child care. The child's age and the amount of time spent in substitute care situations are also contributing factors.

Effects on Parents

In a 1988 report on child care and productivity produced for the Child Care Action Campaign, child care expert Ellen Galinsky posed the following questions: What problems do parents face in arranging and keeping child care, and what impact do these problems have on workers on the job? Galinsky's findings, summarized below, are bolstered by other studies:

1. Child care arrangements can be difficult to find. The Department of Education study cites the availability of regulated care for approximately 6 million children, yet there are over 10 million children under age six whose mothers work. Galinsky's study found that one of the most significant predictors of absenteeism was difficulty finding child care.
2. Parental satisfaction with the type of child care selected varies with the type of arrangement and affects absenteeism and tardiness, and thus productivity.

3. Parents must often make multiple child care arrangements, which can be difficult to maintain. A high rate of turnover in arrangements, lack of care for sick children, and child care breakdowns result in tardiness and absenteeism and affect employees' ability to concentrate on the job. If employed parents have trouble finding or keeping child care, they are more likely to be absent. They are also likely to have higher stress levels and thus more health problems.

The greatest problems are experienced by workers whose children are left to care for themselves. A survey of 8,121 Oregon workers, conducted by Portland State University, found that parents of latch-key children were the workers most affected on the job by missed days, lateness, interruptions, and early departures. Parents with children in self-care missed an average of 13 days per year, compared with an overall average of 7 to 9 days. The highest absenteeism rate for all employees was for men whose children were in self-care.

The Role of Employers in Child Care

In recent years an increasing number of employers have begun to respond to the conflict between work and family responsibilities experienced by the parents of young children. The number of employers who provide child care-related support for their employees grew 400 percent between 1981 and 1991. Some 4,600 of the nation's 6 million employers currently provide some kind of support for child care. Most often this takes the form of educating parents about available options.

Results of several nationwide surveys indicate that employers consistently report the following benefits associated with offering child care services for employees:

- Enhanced recruitment
- Lower absenteeism
- Improved morale
- Lower job turnover rate
- Favorable publicity
- Improved public image
- Improved productivity

Following are descriptions of the findings of major studies (in order of date of publication):

A survey conducted by the National Employer-Supported Child Care Project, published in 1984, found the following:

- 90 percent of the 178 companies responding said that the child care service(s) they provided had improved employee morale.
- 85 percent said their ability to recruit had been affected positively.
- 85 percent reported more positive public relations.
- 83 percent reported higher employee work satisfaction.
- 73 percent reported greater employee commitment.
- 65 percent reported lower turnover.
- 63 percent reported stronger employee motivation.
- 53 percent reported lower absenteeism.
- 50 percent reported increased scheduling flexibility.
- 49 percent reported greater productivity.

During the summer of 1987, the U.S. Bureau of Labor Statistics conducted a nationwide survey of approximately 10,000 business establishments and federal agencies to determine what type of child care services they provided their employees.

Some 11 percent of the establishments with 10 or more employees reported that they provided such direct benefits as employer-sponsored day care, assistance with child care costs, information and referral to community child care resources, counseling services, and/or a variety of other benefits.

About three-fifths of the establishments reported that at least some of their employees could take advantage of indirect benefits in the form of work schedule or leave policies that could aid them in their family obligations. Examples include flextime, flexible leave, and voluntary shifts to part-time work schedules.

The Employee Benefits Survey of medium and large private employers conducted by the Bureau of Labor Statistics found the following as of 1989:

- 5 percent of employees had access to employer assistance for child care.
- 3 percent had access to elder care assistance.
- 11 percent had access to flextime.

- 37 percent had access to unpaid maternity leave.
- 3 percent had access to paid maternity leave.
- 18 percent had access to unpaid paternity leave and 1 percent had access to paid paternity leave.

Forms of Employer Support

Employer response to the changing nature of the work force has taken many forms, with companies that provide child care assistance generally becoming involved by providing one or more of the following:

- Financial assistance
- Information services
- Direct services
- Flexible personnel policies

Most companies opt to develop a combination of programs to meet the needs of their employees while effectively maintaining the efficiency and effectiveness of the organization. According to the Women's Bureau, benefit availability varies by size of business. Smaller businesses (10–49 employees) were more likely to provide some of the flexible work schedule policies. Large establishments (250 employees or more) were more likely to provide direct child care benefits such as sponsorship of a child care center.

Here are brief descriptions of child care–related employer options:

Financial Assistance Options

Voucher/Reimbursement System: An employee selects a child care program and submits an employer-financed voucher to the provider, covering all or part of the cost of services. This option gives parents full responsibility for choosing their own child care providers.

Vendor Program: The employer reserves or purchases spaces in existing child care programs for employees' use. Employees usually cover the cost of providing care. Often arrangements are made between the employer and a child care center for employees to purchase care at discounted rates. Employers may choose to make up the difference in cost.

Dependent Care Assistance Program (DCAP): As a tax-exempt employee benefit, employers offer a child care "allowance." The company must prepare a written plan to ensure that DCAP allowances are nondiscriminatory, both in eligibility and in provision of benefits.

As described in Section 129 of the Internal Revenue Code, a DCAP recognizes dependent care services as a fringe benefit not considered as taxable income, allowing an employer to assist in child care services. Since the DCAP is not considered part of the employee's salary, the employee does not pay federal income or social security taxes on the amount of assistance.

The maximum qualified expenses for the child care tax credit are $2,400 for one child and $4,800 for two or more children. The maximum DCAP allowance is $5,000 for one or more children. The DCAP becomes more advantageous when the costs for one child are between $2,400 and $5,000. A parent cannot claim the child care tax credit in addition to using a DCAP unless total child care expenditures exceed $5,000.

Flexible Spending Account/Salary Redirection Plan: The federal government allows employers to provide up to $5,000 a year in assistance on a tax-deductible basis for both the employer and the employee. Designated expenses include medical, dependent child care, and personal/legal expenditures. Money can come from three sources: employer contributions, trade-off with other benefits in a flexible benefits plan, or from the employee through salary redirection. Only eligible expenses are reimbursed, and whatever amount remains in the account at the end of the year is forfeited.

Information Services

Parent Education Seminars: Staff or outside consultants organize forums to inform working parents about community resources and to provide support on work and family issues. Groups may be held at the work site during lunch hours or at other appropriate times.

Resource and Referral (R&R) Services: Employers may establish in-house services or contract with national or local resource and referral agencies to provide services to employees. There has been a surge of growth in R&Rs in the last decade, with approximately 60 identified in the 1980s and more than 300 by the early 1990s. Nearly half the states have formed statewide Child Care Resource & Referral Networks, including Alabama, Alaska, California, Colorado, Florida, Illinois, Michigan, Minnesota, New York, Ohio, Oregon, Texas, Virginia, and Washington.

The following are among the services provided by R&R agencies:

- Educate parents about the elements of quality child care and support them in their efforts to locate care and improve quality.
- Track program vacancies and provide detailed program information about each service in response to parent requests.
- Document child care supply and demand in the service area, in order to support community planning efforts.
- Provide technical assistance and training to new and experienced providers.
- Improve the supply and retention of high-quality child care providers via recruitment and by addressing the retention issue.
- Consult with employers on child care-related issues.

Direct Services

On-Site or Near-Site Centers: These are child care facilities established at the workplace or at a site located convenient to the workplace. Employers may own and operate their own child care facilities, or they may contract with for-profit or not-for-profit organizations to run centers for company employees. Currently, approximately 1,800 employers of all sizes offer some form of child care provision that is located at or near the workplace site.

Consortium Centers: A child care center may be set up by a collaborating group of employers, a consortium, who share the costs and benefits of establishing it. This type of option is popular in industrial parks, shopping malls, and downtown business districts.

Sick Child Care Programs: This option offers support to employees whose children are mildly ill or who are recovering from health problems. Programs can be provided in several ways, including a "sick bay" in a child care center (allowed in some states), a hospital-based program, a center specializing in drop-in care for mildly ill children, in-home services such as visiting nurses, or family child care homes recruited by the company to care for ill children of employees. Because the cost of such programs can also be prohibitive for employees, a growing number of companies subsidize some portion of fees related to the purchase of sick care.

Family Child Care Network: Employers establish and/or help to support a network of family child care homes to provide child care for employees. Support may include recruitment and training of providers, centralized purchasing of supplies, liability insurance, access to company benefits, and financial and in-kind support. Usually, family child care homes are evaluated before being admitted to a network, and providers receive training and support services such as monthly workshops, newsletters, and access to a toy-lending library. A family child care network can be a useful solution for situations requiring overnight and/or odd-hours care.

Flexible Personnel Policies

Flextime: Employees choose the time they arrive at work and the time they leave, as long as they accumulate the required number of hours per day or week.

Voluntary Reduced Time: Employees may reduce their work time and pay by 5–50 percent for a specified period, usually 6 to 12 months. Workers retain their benefits and seniority status on a prorated basis. Companies have begun to offer this option to help employees meet family needs, as well as to provide an alternative to layoffs.

Job Sharing: Two compatible workers share the responsibilities and wages of one full-time job.

Compressed Workweek: Employees complete the number of hours for a pay period in less than the full pay period. For example, employees work a 40-hour week in four 10-hour days, rather than the traditional five 8-hour days a week.

Flexplace/Telecommuting: Employees work in places outside their employers' establishments, such as at home or at a satellite work site.

Parental Leave: An extended period of time off is allowed for mothers or fathers to care for newborn or very young children. Under the 1978 Pregnancy Discrimination Act (PDA), employers are required to adhere to two basic guidelines:

1. Employers must permit physically fit pregnant employees to continue to work, just as they would any other physically fit employee.
2. Employers must provide the same sick leave, disability, health insurance, or other benefits extended to physically disabled employees to women who become physically unable to work due

to complications of pregnancy, childbirth, and/or recovery following childbirth.

Although comprehensive federal legislation regarding parental leave is still pending, 30 states have established their own widely varying policies. In June 1990, the Women's Bureau of the U.S. Department of Labor reported the following:

Among states offering some form of maternity leave (defined as the time when the mother is on leave for disability as a result of pregnancy, childbirth, or the care of the newborn or newly adopted child) are Massachusetts, Tennessee, and Vermont.

Among states offering some form of parental leave (defined as the time when the mother or father is on leave to care for the newborn or newly adopted child) are California, Connecticut, Illinois, Maine, Maryland, Minnesota, New Jersey, North Dakota, Oklahoma, Oregon, Pennsylvania, Rhode Island, Washington, West Virginia, and Wisconsin.

Among states offering some form of maternity disability leave (defined as only the time when the mother is disabled as a result of pregnancy and childbirth) are Arizona, California, Colorado, Florida, Hawaii, Iowa, Kansas, Louisiana, and Montana.

There is no nationally mandated maternity leave policy in the United States. This is in sharp contrast to policies in other countries. For example:

- France: 16 weeks of full-pay maternity leave and up to two years unpaid leave
- Germany: 14 weeks of full-pay maternity leave and an additional 10 to 12 months at reduced pay
- Sweden: 12 months of leave at 90 percent wage compensation
- Japan: 12 weeks of leave at 60 percent pay

Stages of Employer Involvement

The most recent, and perhaps most comprehensive, study was conducted by Ellen Galinsky and Dana Friedman of the Families and Work Institute. The results of a survey of the largest Fortune 1000 companies in 30 industry areas were published in 1991 in *The Corporate Reference Guide to Work-Family Programs*. From this survey, Galinsky and Friedman studied 188 companies using their Family-Friendly Index, a tool they developed to compare corporate work-family policies and programs. The researchers investigated the following types of programs:

Flextime

Part-time

Work/job sharing

Parental leave

Flexible benefits (with company subsidy to DCAP)

Corporate giving funds to benefit employees

On- or near-site child care center

Work-family management training

Vouchers for dependent care

Child care resource and referral

Elder care consultation and referral

Consortium child care centers

Flexplace

Sick/emergency child care programs

After-school programs

Summer camps

Work-family coordinators

Wellness/health promotion

Long-term care insurance

Adoption assistance

Work-family handbooks

Employee assistance programs (EAPs)

Relocation services

Work-family seminars

Work-family support groups

Work-family newsletters

Child care discounts

Caregiver fairs

An analysis of the resultant data identified three distinct stages of employer involvement in child care issues:

> *Stage 1:* One or more internal child care advocates begin to build a case for addressing child care concerns as a means of countering lost productivity on the job. At this point child care is viewed by upper management primarily as a women's issue, and equity for all employees is seen as a major barrier to employer involvement. Programs adopted by companies in this stage revolve around flexible time schedules, flexible benefits, and child care assistance.

> *Stage 2:* Work and family issues are integrated into the company's human resource area and are focused on the real needs of the company's employee base. Next, upper management "buys into" the concept of corporate commitment to work and family concerns. The emphasis of work-family policies and programs is enlarged beyond child care to include issues such as elder care and relocation. A package of policies and programs is developed in response to a demographically assessed set of work-family issues.

> *Stage 3:* At this "mature" stage of development, work and family issues are mainstreamed into corporate culture and aligned with other human resource issues. Work and family issues become linked to strategic business planning and bottom-line impact.

Scrutiny under the Family-Friendly Index revealed that more than three-fourths of the companies surveyed had not passed Stage 1. The following four companies were determined to be the family-friendliest: Johnson & Johnson, IBM, Aetna Life and Casualty, and Corning.

Small Business Involvement

As employers to more than 50 percent of the female labor force, many small businesses have also come to realize the importance of effective work-family strategies in attracting and retaining valuable personnel, improving productivity and morale, and enhancing community image. In its 1991 report, *Not Too Small To Care,* the Child Care Action Campaign (CCAC) profiles 29 businesses employing fewer than 250 workers in 15 states. This research presents innovative employersponsored child care programs that illustrate the major role small business can play in resolving work-family conflicts.

The CCAC study indicates that current small business child care programs and policies revolve around five key areas:

1. Direct provision of licensed child care—either on-site or off-site—through a child care center or family child care homes
2. Child care subsidies paid directly to the parent or the child care provider
3. Implementation of a dependent care assistance program
4. Provision of resource and referral services
5. Development of a flexible benefits plan

Cost of Child Care

Child care is expensive. According to the Children's Defense Fund, the average cost for one year of full-time care for one child is $3,432, a price tag that many families find difficult to absorb. The cost varies according to locale, with parents in major metropolitan areas paying considerably more than the average. For instance, the average annual cost of child care in New York City is $8,944. In Boston, child care runs an average of $5,668 annually, while in San Francisco it costs $4,264 and in Chicago, $3,900. Milwaukee averages $3,536, Los Angeles $3,484, and Miami reports a below-average cost of $2,964.

The data also support the theory that the poor pay a higher percentage of their income for child care than those in higher income brackets. For instance, employed mothers who earn an annual income below $15,000 spend nearly 21 percent of their income on child care (an amount comparable to housing expenditures), while the average cost of child care for women earning more than $45,000 is slightly less than 5 percent (comparable to food expenditures).

Census data also reveal that the price of child care varies with the age of the child. For example, employed mothers with children under the age of 1 year spend an average of $58.10 per week on child care, amounting to 8 percent of annual income, while those with children age 5 and over spend an average of $36.60 a week, amounting to 4.5 percent of annual income.

Provider Compensation

While the cost of child care can be high for parents, this does not necessarily translate into high or even average salaries for child care providers. The findings of the National Child Care Staffing Study indicate that child care center workers are paid significantly less than their counterparts in the civilian labor force with similar education. Thus the cost of child care is kept artificially low by the dedicated people—almost always women—who provide it. Given that staff wages account for 60–80 percent of the operating costs of a child care center, providers' low salaries help subsidize the cost of care.

The following is a comparison of the average wages earned by child care workers with the incomes of other civilian employees, compiled as a result of the National Child Care Staffing Study:

With high school diploma or less

   Child care worker: $8,120

   Average labor force, women: $15,806

   Average labor force, men: $24,097

With some college

   Child care worker: $9,293

   Average labor force, women: $19,369

   Average labor force, men: $29,251

With B.A./B.S. or more

   Child care worker: $11,603

   Average labor force, women: $26,006

   Average labor force, men: $42,422

In its 1989 National Child Care Staffing Study, the Child Care Employee Project found that staff wages and teacher education levels are two important predictors of quality child care, and that high staff turnover rate is directly related to low wages. The turnover rate for child care providers was 48 percent overall in 1988, compared with the average turnover rate for all occupations of about 18 percent. Turnover makes it difficult to provide children with continuity of care, which in turn jeopardizes quality.

When asked to recommend strategies to improve child care quality, teachers participating in the Child Care Staffing Study responded with the following suggestions:

- Better salaries for child care work
- Improved benefits
- Increased social respect for child care work
- Ongoing or continuing education
- A career ladder in child care
- An environment that values adults as well as children

Quality of Child Care Services

Defining Quality Child Care

The National Association for the Education of Young Children defines a quality child care program as one that meets the needs of and promotes the physical, social, emotional, and cognitive development of the children and adults—parents, staff, and administrators—who are involved in the program. Each day of a child's life is viewed as leading toward the growth and development of a healthy, intelligent, and contributing member of society.

The Children's Defense Fund lists the following criteria, which most professional organizations, federal agencies, academic agencies, and parents would agree are essential components of high-quality care:

- A nurturing, well-trained, and stable staff that has time to interact with and develop relationships with the children
- Good health, nutrition, and safety practices
- An appropriate and safe physical environment
- Developmentally appropriate curricula
- Parental involvement and access
- Parental choice and satisfaction
- Cultural sensitivity

In one of the most comprehensive child care studies ever done in the United States, the National Day Care Study (also known as the Abt Study), researchers seeking to determine the quality of child care centers used a set of environmental variables that have come to be known as the "iron triangle." The three factors determined to play an important role in quality child care are as follows:

1. Group size: Findings consistently favor small groups.
2. Caregiver:child ratio: Findings on ratios for infants and toddlers are more consistent than findings for preschoolers.
3. Caregiver qualifications: The focus is on education and training in child development and experience in child care.

Indicators of Quality Child Care

Minimal Staff:Child Ratios

As is evident from the following, the "ideal" staff:child ratios suggested by recognized child care authorities are similar, but not identical. According to the Early Childhood Environment Rating Scale, the ratios should be as follows:

Infants or toddlers: 1 to 3–4

3-year-olds: 1 to 7–8

5-year-olds: 1 to 8–10

The National Association for the Education of Young Children recommends the following ratios:

1-year-olds: 1 to 3–4

3-year-olds: 1 to 7–10

5-year-olds: 1 to 8–10

And the Child Welfare League of America gives these ratios:

1-year-olds: 1 to 4

3-year-olds: 1 to 5

5-year-olds: 1 to 7

Interactions among Staff and Children

In high-quality child care environments, the following elements are characteristic of the interactions among staff and children:

- Staff interact frequently with children, showing affection and respect.
- Staff are responsive to children.
- Staff speak with children in a friendly, courteous manner.
- Staff encourage independence in children as they are ready for it.
- Staff use positive approaches to help children behave constructively.
- Staff do not use physical punishment or other negative discipline methods that hurt, frighten, or humiliate children.
- Staff encourage prosocial behaviors in children, such as cooperating, helping, taking turns, and talking to solve problems.
- Staff expectations of children's social behavior are developmentally appropriate.
- Children are encouraged to talk about feelings and ideas instead of solving problems with force.

Curriculum

High-quality child care includes the following curricular elements:

- The daily schedule provides a balance of indoor and outdoor activities.
- The daily schedule provides a balance of quiet and active activities.
- Developmentally appropriate materials and equipment are available for infants, toddlers, and/or preschoolers.
- Staff provide a variety of developmentally appropriate hands-on activities to encourage language development.
- Staff provide a variety of developmentally appropriate hands-on activities to enhance physical development.
- Staff provide a variety of developmentally appropriate hands-on activities to foster positive self-concept.
- Staff provide a variety of developmentally appropriate hands-on activities to develop social skills.

Physical Environment

The environment of a high-quality child care center should include the following:

- There is a minimum of 35 square feet of usable playroom floor space per child indoors.

- There is a minimum of 75 square feet of play space outdoors per child (when space is in use).
- The center is licensed or accredited by the appropriate state/local agencies. If exempt from licensing, the center demonstrates compliance with its own state's regulations.

Health and Safety

The health and safety of children are safeguarded in high-quality child care environments:

- Toileting and diapering areas are sanitary.
- Staff wash their hands with soap and water before feeding, preparing, or serving food, and after diapering or assisting children with toileting or nose wiping.
- A sink with running hot and cold water is very close to diapering and toileting areas.
- The building, play yard, and all equipment are maintained in safe, clean condition and in good repair.
- Infants' and toddlers' toys are large enough to prevent swallowing or choking.
- Sides of infants' cribs are in a locked position when cribs are occupied.
- Toilets, drinking water, and hand-washing facilities are easily accessible to children.
- Soap and disposable towels are provided.
- Children wash hands after toileting and before meals.

Warning Signs of Poor Child Care

In a Child Care Action Campaign fact sheet, Thelma Harms lists the following indicators as potential danger signs:

1. Parents are not allowed to drop in unannounced at all times of the day. Parents are required to call before coming to pick up their children at different times or before visiting.
2. Parents must drop off their children in the office and may not go into the caregiving areas.
3. After several months, a child continues to be unhappy about going to the day care facility, or a child suddenly becomes unhappy after he or she seems to have adjusted.
4. Children talk about being afraid of or disliking a particular caregiver, or seem quiet and fearful in her presence.
5. There is frequent staff turnover.

6. The care seems lax or indifferent. Children are made to wait for long periods of time or are left to play unattended indoors or outdoors.
7. Children have an excessive number of injuries that the caregiver cannot explain adequately.
8. The caregiver's voice or manner seems harsh, rude, or indifferent toward any of the children.
9. There are insufficient toys for the children to play with or few interesting activities to do. Toys may be put on display but not used regularly by the children.
10. When parental concerns are expressed, the caregiver becomes upset or defensive and cannot discuss the matter rationally with the parent.

State Child Care Standards

Regulations alone cannot guarantee quality child care. However, government regulations can create child care environments that are conducive to high-quality child care. According to child care advocate Gwen Morgan, "State and federal regulations can establish a basic floor of quality, the ceiling is established by the goals of the child care provider."

The federal government's attempt to establish child care regulations, Federal Interagency Day Care Requirements, was permanently suspended by legislative action in 1981. It has thus fallen to each state to interpret what is deemed adequate in terms of child care regulations. Not surprisingly, state-mandated standards for child care establishments vary widely and often do not meet even the minimum criteria recommended by child care experts, as illustrated by the following:

- In 22 states it is permissible for five or more babies to be cared for in child care centers by a single staff member without an assistant, and at least 10 states permit day care providers to care for five or more babies alone.
- In 29 states and the District of Columbia there is no guarantee that parents can drop in unannounced at their children's child care centers.
- In 21 states and the District of Columbia there are no requirements concerning any form of training for family day care providers.
- In 23 states and the District of Columbia there are no specific requirements for ongoing training of child care center staff.

Accreditation

Accreditation is a tool used to evaluate the quality of a given child care situation and provider. The accreditation process is used to identify and distinguish those providers reaching a specified level of professional competence and experience.

In measuring the quality of family child care, three national accreditation tools are widely used:

- The Child Development Associate (CDA) Competency Standards
- The National Association for Family Day Care Assessment Profile (NAFDC)
- The Harms-Clifford Family Day Care Rating Scale (FDCRS)

According to Kathy Modigliani in her report *Assessing the Quality of Child Care,* several benefits of accreditation have been reported:

- It identifies standards of quality (standards that are higher than the minimal standards of state regulations).
- It gives professional recognition to deserving providers.
- It creates incentives for providers to improve their businesses and child development practices.
- It is helpful for parents who are looking for quality child care.
- It draws providers into training and continuing education.

The Role of the Government in Child Care

From the end of World War II until very recently, child care has not been a national legislative priority. The last comprehensive national child care program to be enacted was the Lantham Act (P.L. 137) in 1941, which authorized funding for the establishment of centers in defense plants to provide care for the children of women working in the war effort.

In 1971, President Nixon vetoed the last major child care proposal to pass Congress. Recently, however, the sheer number of families requiring some form of child care support in order to maintain economic self-sufficiency has brought the issue into the spotlight, forcing legislators on every level to recognize the need for government involvement.

Recent attempts to implement child care legislation have run into widely divergent philosophies that fall along political party lines. Among the many issues that have been discussed during the lengthy legislative process are the following:

- The extent to which Congress should impose child care standards on the states
- The constitutionality of providing federal funds to religious child care providers
- The best way to provide assistance to needy families

The role of government in child care is currently being discussed on many fronts. Many oppose any form of government intervention as an infringement of parental rights and choice in the selection of child care services. Further, an estimated one-fourth to one-third of existing child care centers are housed in religious facilities, making the issue of separation of church and state a major consideration. In response to such concerns, the Child Care Action Campaign released a fact sheet outlining the following principles regarding government involvement in child care:

All children should have access to affordable, quality child care. Child care must be of quality sufficient to ensure that children get the education, social, and health benefits that are essential to growth at each and every stage of development.

Every sector that benefits from child care should invest in it—families; federal, state, and local governments; and employers. This would avoid a two-tiered system in which only children of those who can afford it receive quality child care.

Parents/caregivers should have access to adequate professional information about existing resources, various alternatives, and the components of quality care in order to be able to make informed choices for their families.

Parents must play an integral part in any child care program, so that their values are communicated to their children. Programs must respect cultural differences.

There should be a variety of quality, affordable options for family care so that caregivers anywhere in the nation can choose the type best suited to their needs and values and to those for whom they are caring.

Family care funding should be administered in a manner designed to maximize coordination and efficient use of resources. Duplication of programs and turf battles must be eliminated or minimized.

Resources for family care must be planned for and coordinated through a partnership of different levels of government: federal, state, and local. The state should ensure that there is a continuum of care, that caregivers can make informed choices among a variety of options, and that the resources invested are effectively used. The federal government should set standards or act as facilitator and clearinghouse.

All levels of government must create plans and strategies to develop public-private partnerships to resolve the family care crisis.

Because child care providers are the most essential component of quality, training, wages, benefits, and working conditions must be improved so that competent and caring providers are attracted to the profession and are able to remain in it.

Child Care Philosophy of the Bush Administration

In order to gain a better understanding of the rationale behind recent national child care legislation, it is helpful to have some insight into the child care philosophy of the current presidential administration. In describing President Bush's child care philosophy to the Senate Committee on Finance in April 1989, Secretary of Labor Elizabeth Dole emphasized the following guiding principles:

1. There is a recognition of the differing circumstances of today's families and the need to offer parents a choice in the type of child care best suited to their needs.
2. Federal policy should increase, not decrease, the range of options available to parents. Federal policy should expand the range of choices available to parents, not limit them through biasing federal support toward one kind of care (especially in terms of church-sponsored or family member care).
3. The federal government should not discriminate against those families who sacrifice the income of a second career for one parent to stay at home to care for their children.
4. Assistance should be targeted to low-income families.

Recent Child Care Legislation

Act for Better Child Care Services

The Act for Better Child Care Services of 1989, commonly referred to as the ABC Bill, was introduced by Senator Christopher Dodd (D-CT) in January 1989. It would have provided federal funding for direct child care services, federally mandated child care standards for states created by a child care commission, and many other licensing, inspection, and training requirements. After revisions by Senator Orrin Hatch (R-UT) and additions of a tax credit package and child health insurance credit by Senator Lloyd Bentsen (D-TX), the bill failed to get the necessary Senate votes to take it to the House of Representatives. President Bush had threatened to veto the bill if it passed.

Omnibus Budget Reconciliation Act of 1990

The dialogue and momentum created by the ABC Bill kept child care in a priority position during the next legislative session, and the 101st Congress finally agreed to a comprehensive child care package. The lessons learned during the ABC Bill process resulted in a series of compromises and adjustments that were ultimately passed as part of the Omnibus Reconciliation Act (OBRA; P.L. 101-508). The final child care package contains four parts:

- The Child Care and Development Block Grant
- The Earned Income Tax Credit (EITC) expansions
- A child care entitlement added to Title IV-A of the Social Security Act
- Child Care Licensing Improvement Grants under Title IV-A

Child Care and Development Block Grant.   OBRA 1990 authorizes $2.5 billion over the next three years to assist states in helping families pay for child care, in improving and expanding the supply, and in helping schools and community-based child care organizations provide before- and after-school care and early childhood education programs. Funding is authorized as follows:

- $750 million in fiscal year 1991
- $825 million in fiscal year 1992
- $925 million in fiscal year 1993
- Funding as necessary in fiscal years 1994 and 1995

No state matching funds are required. The state allocation formula is based on three factors:

- Number of children under the age of 5
- Number of children receiving free or reduced-price school lunch
- Per capita income

Three-fourths of the block grant funds are designated for use in providing child care to families with children under the age of 13 and incomes below 75 percent of the state median income. Direct assistance funds are available on a sliding fee scale basis and require that parents select a licensed, regulated, or registered provider that is in compliance with applicable state and local laws.

The remaining 25 percent of the block grant funds is designated to improve quality of child care, early childhood development, and before- and after-school services, in these amounts:

5 percent for quality improvement, including investment in resource and referral programs, assistance in meeting state and local standards, monitoring of compliance with licensing and regulatory requirements, provider training, and provider salary enhancement

18.75 percent to increase the availability of early childhood development and before- and after-school services

1.25 percent may be used for either category at the individual state's discretion

Under the law, states must establish health and safety standards for providers. They may impose more stringent requirements on providers receiving grant money. Each state is to conduct a one-time review of its child care licensing policies and regulations. States must report to secretary of Health and Human Services, who in turn must make an annual report to Congress.

Earned Income Tax Credit. OBRA 1990 includes provisions to expand the EITC for low-income working families and adjust it for family size, to provide an additional credit for families with children under 1 year of age, and to provide a child health insurance tax credit. The EITC differs from the Dependent Care Tax Credit in that a family need not have child care expenses to receive the Earned Income Tax Credit.

This provision accounts for the largest share of funding, at an estimated $12.4 billion in tax expenditures over five years.

In 1994, after a three-year phase-in process, the EITC for eligible families with one child will be 23 percent of earnings up to $6,810 (increased from the 14 percent allowed under previous law). For eligible families with more than one child, the credit will be 25 percent. An additional 5 percent credit will be available for taxpayers with a child under age 1. In addition, a 6 percent credit will be available for eligible families purchasing qualified health insurance for their children.

Title IV-A Child Care Grants.   Also included in OBRA 1990 is a five-year $1.5 billion child care entitlement program under Title IV-A. An amount of $300 million was permanently authorized for the program beginning in 1991. The Title IV-A program will operate as a "capped entitlement," under which states are entitled to matching funds for child care expenditures up to state limits determined by formula.

Title IV-A already provides funds for a number of important programs for low-income families, including child care services for recipients of Aid to Families with Dependent Children (AFDC) who are participating in education or job training programs. The funds authorized in the reconciliation package make child care available to any family the state determines is not on AFDC, needs child care in order to work, and is at risk of becoming dependent on AFDC.

Title IV-A Child Care Licensing Improvement Grants.   OBRA 1990 amends and extends this existing program, under which states receive 90 percent federal matching funds through a formula in law for improving their child care licensing and registration requirements, enforcing standards, and providing training to child care providers. It also amends the program to add other functions, including provider training. The bill authorizes funding for the program of $50 million annually for 1992 through 1994. Under the new provisions, states must spend 50 percent of their grants on provider training.

Church-State Provisions.   Funds provided to states under the Child Care and Development Block Grant program may not be used for any sectarian purpose. However, parents may use child care certificates provided under the program to purchase child care from religious child care providers.

Providers receiving assistance under the block grant program cannot discriminate on religious grounds with respect to either admission of children or hiring practices for employees who work directly with children. However, religious providers who receive less than 80 percent of their operating budgets from public funds may discriminate on religious grounds with respect to all of their employees.

According to the Congressional Research Service, there are no restrictions under the Title IV-A child care grants programs regarding sectarian use or nondiscrimination.

Human Services Reauthorization Act of 1990

Under the Human Services Reauthorization Act of 1984 (P.L. 98-558), the federal government provided grant funds for the planning, development, establishment, expansion, and improvement of dependent-care resource and referral services and school-age child care services. The act required a 25 percent match in state or local funds. The Augustus F. Hawkins Human Services Reauthorization Act of 1990 (H.R. 4151, P.L. 101-501) extends through 1994 the following two programs established in the 1984 law:

1. The State Dependent Care Development Grants program, which funds school-age child care and resource and referral programs. The law amends the grant program to permit states to fund operational as well as start-up costs for these programs.
2. The Child Development Associate (CDA) Scholarship Assistance Act. The law amends this act to allow states to use up to 35 percent of funds to cover the cost of training associated with the CDA credential. It also raises the eligibility level to 130 percent of the lower living standard.

The Family and Medical Leave Act

In 1991, the Senate voted 65 to 32 (enough to override a presidential veto) in favor of a compromise version of the Family and Medical Leave Act, S.5, which would allow workers to take time off from their jobs in times of family emergency. The Bond-Ford compromise measure provides up to 12 weeks of job-protected, unpaid leave to workers needing time off for the birth of a new child or for serious family illnesses. Coverage is limited to employers with more than 50 workers. The House voted 253–177 in favor of a similar measure. At this writing, the bill is scheduled to go before a House-Senate conference committee.

The bill requires employees to provide 30 days' notice to the employer of their intent to take leave in cases of birth, adoption, or planned medical treatments. Employees who fail to return to work may be required to repay medical insurance premiums paid by the employer during the leave. The estimated cost to business is $6 per employee.

Child Care–Related Government Programs

Dependent Care Tax Credit

The Dependent Care Tax Credit allows families to deduct from their federal taxes expenditures for the care of children under the age of 15 or dependents of any age, including spouses, who are physically or mentally incapable of caring for themselves. The amount of the credit is determined by the adjusted gross income shown on the family's federal income tax return; the maximum credit is $2,400 for one child and $4,800 for two or more children. In 1986, more than 8.4 million taxpayers claimed the Dependent Care Tax Credit, accounting for $3.1 billion in tax credits. The OBRA child care package did not make any changes to the Dependent Care Tax Credit, currently available to all working families with children under age 15.

Child Care Food Program

Under the Child Care Food Program (CCFP), the U.S. Department of Agriculture distributes funds to provide nutritious meals to low-income children enrolled in child care centers and family day care homes. Facilities eligible for the program include tax-exempt organizations and private for-profit centers that receive compensation under the Social Services Block Grant for at least 25 percent of the children in their care. All programs receiving funds through the CCFP must be licensed or approved.

Head Start

Head Start is a direct program subsidy addressing compensatory education needs of children whose families fall below the federal government's poverty guidelines. It was created to provide a quality early childhood education program in order to help break the cycle of poverty. The program provides educational, social, medical, and nutritional services to low-income preschool children, usually between the ages of 3 and 5.

Although it is a federally funded child development program, Head Start is locally administered by education agencies, community action agencies, and public and private not-for-profit organizations. Head Start funds are allocated to states on the basis of a formula that takes into account each state's annual fiscal allocations and the proportion of children in families receiving AFDC residing in the state. In recent years, funding for the program has increased modestly. In fiscal 1989, just over $1 billion was distributed directly to Head Start programs serving approximately 450,000 children, 20 percent of those eligible.

School-Age Child Care

Under the Human Services Reauthorization Act in 1986, a total of $4,785,000 was distributed to states and territories for the planning, development, establishment, expansion, and improvement of school-age child care services. The funds were distributed according to state populations. Each grant required a 25 percent match from state or local funds. School-age child care programs may also use funds provided by the USDA for the school breakfast program.

Return on Investment in Child Care

The House Select Committee on Children, Youth and Families found that each dollar invested in preschool education returns $4.75 through savings in special education and welfare. The Children's Defense Fund estimates that for every dollar invested in high-quality preschool programs, $6.00 is saved because of decreased need for expenditures related to remediation and crime.

Slowly but surely, American decision makers are coming to recognize the wisdom and cost-effectiveness of providing a foundation from which parents can do a good job of raising and supporting their families, business can prosper, and children can flourish.

Sources

Abt Associates. *Day Care Centers in the U.S.: A National Profile, 1976–77.* Cambridge, MA: 1979.

Burund, S., P. Aschbacher, and J. McCroskey. *Employer Supported Child Care: Investing in Human Resources.* Boston: Auburn House, 1984.

Center for Policy Research, National Governor's Association. *Taking Care: State Developments in Child Care.* Washington, DC: National Governor's Association, 1990.

Child Care Action Campaign. *Child Care ActioNews,* November-December 1990.

———. *Not Too Small To Care: Small Businesses and Child Care.* New York: 1991.

———. *Wages and Benefits in Child Care* (Information Guide No. 16). New York:

Children's Defense Fund. *A Vision for America's Future.* Washington, DC: 1989.

———. *The Nation's Investment in Children.* Washington, DC: 1991.

Congressional Caucus for Women's Issues. *Update on Women and Family Issues in Congress.* Washington, DC: October 2, 1991.

Fernandez, John. *Child Care and Corporate Productivity: Resolving Family/Work Conflicts.* Lexington, MA: Lexington Books, 1986.

Friedman, Dana. "Child Care for Employees' Kids." *Harvard Business Review,* March-April 1986.

Galinsky, Ellen. *Child Care and Productivity.* New York: Child Care Action Campaign, 1988.

——— and Dana Friedman. *The Corporate Reference Guide to Work-Family Programs.* New York: Families and Work Institute, 1991.

Harms, Thelma. *Warning Signs of Poor Child Care* (Fact Sheet No. 29). New York: Child Care Action Campaign.

——— and Richard Clifford. *Early Childhood Environment Rating Scale.* New York: Teachers College Press, 1980.

Hayes, Cheryl D., John L. Palmer, and Martha J. Zaslow. *Who Cares for America's Children?* Washington, DC: National Academy Press, 1990.

Hofferth, Sandra. *What Is the Demand and Supply of Child Care in the United States? Young Children.* Washington, DC: National Association for the Education of Young Children, July 1989.

Howes, Carollee, Marcy Whitebook, and Deborah Phillips. *Who Cares? Child Care Teachers and the Quality of Care in America.* Oakland, CA: Child Care Employee Project, 1989.

Hudson Institute. *Workforce 2000: Work and Workers for the 21st Century*. Washington, DC: U.S. Department of Labor, 1987.

Kahn, Alfred, and Sheila Kammerman. *Child Care: Facing the Hard Choices*. Boston: Auburn House, 1987.

Modigliani, Kathy. *Assessing the Quality of Family Child Care: An Assessment of Five Instruments*. New York: Bank Street College of Education, 1991.

Morse, Ann, and Sheri Steisel. *Child Care: A Summary and Analysis of New Federal Programs and Tax Credits*. Denver: National Conference of State Legislators, 1990.

National Center for Clinical Infant Programs. *Infants, Families, and Child Care: Toward a Research Agency*. Washington, DC: National Center for Clinical Infant Programs, 1988.

Stewart, Anne C. *CRS Issue Brief: Child Day Care*. Washington, DC: U.S. Government Printing Office, 1990.

U.S. Department of Commerce, Bureau of the Census. *Who's Minding the Kids?* (Current Population Reports, Series P-70, No. 9). Washington, DC: U.S. Department of Commerce, 1987.

U.S. Department of Labor. *Facts about Working Women*. Washington, DC: 1988.

———. *Employers and Child Care: Benefiting Work and Family*. Washington, DC: Women's Bureau, 1989.

———. *Facts on Working Women*. Washington, DC: 1989.

———. *Facts on Working Women*. Washington, DC: Women's Bureau, June 1990.

U.S. Department of Labor, Bureau of Labor Statistics. *Marital and Family Characteristics of the Labor Force*. Washington, DC: U.S. Department of Labor, March 1988.

———. *Report on Employer Child Care Practices*. Washington, DC: U.S. Department of Labor, 1988.

U.S. House of Representatives, Select Committee on Children, Youth, and Families. *Babies and Briefcases: Creating a Family-Friendly Workplace for Fathers*. Washington, DC: U.S. House of Representatives, May 1991.

Zigler, Edward F., and Mary C. Lang. *Child Care Choices: Balancing the Needs of Children, Family and Society*. New York: Macmillan, 1991.

Zinmeister, Karl. "Hard Truths about Day Care." *Policy Review*, Spring 1988.

4

Directory of
Organizations

FOLLOWING ARE DESCRIPTIONS of major national child care support organizations. These organizations fulfill different roles in the child care arena—while some are devoted strictly to the delivery of some form of child care support, others are child-serving organizations that have found it important to address child care issues.

The diversity of the services offered by these organizations bears testament to the fact that child care is not simply "baby-sitting." This compilation of organizations includes comprehensive resources for employers, parents, child care providers, and resource and referral agencies.

American Child Care Foundation (ACCF)
1801 Robert Fulton Drive, Suite 400
Reston, VA 22091
(703) 758-3583

Description: The American Child Care Foundation is a nonprofit, tax-exempt organization dedicated to promoting the development of a broad range of quality child care services in the following ways: increasing public awareness of the need for affordable, quality child care services in the United States, contributing to the development of high standards for child care services, supporting the dissemination of information on the development and management of quality child care services, increasing the availability of well-trained child care workers for all phases of child care, improving the image and professional status of child care workers, and conducting and supporting research on child care and child development issues. Services available through ACCF include seminars designed for employers, child care professionals, and/or parents; an annual training and networking conference for school-age child care professionals; and publications and audio-visual resources on child care and child development issues.

Publications: A bimonthly newsletter, *Caring Families,* is aimed at helping parents create harmony and balance in their lives at work and at home.

Bank Street College
Work and Family Life Studies
Division of Research Demonstration, and Policy
610 West 112th Street
New York, NY 10025
(212) 875-4651

Description: Through a combination of action research, demonstration projects, and policy analysis, Bank Street's Division of Research, Demonstration, and Policy seeks to improve developmental opportunities for children and adolescents and to enhance family functioning. Current projects are clustered in three areas: early childhood, school improvement, and youth at risk by virtue of poverty or other handicapping conditions. Two early childhood-related projects are centered on examining the role public schools and the child care community play in meeting the needs of preschool children and working parents and on studying the challenges related to recruiting and retaining teachers for preschool children. Bank Street College also offers bachelor's- and master's-level programs in early childhood leadership and day care management.

Publications: Recent reports include *Between Promise and Practice,* an analysis of early childhood issues related to the role of the public school in early childhood programs, and *Home Is Where the Heart Is,* a study of New York City homeless preschool children.

Catalyst
250 Park Avenue South
New York, NY 10003-1459
(212) 777-8900

Description: The main function of this national not-for-profit organization is to work with business to effect change for women—through research, advisory services, and communications. The organization's role in child care takes the form of seeking solutions that benefit both families and business and educating business leaders about options and responsibilities in this vital workplace issue.

Membership: Corporate contributors become eligible for access to the Catalyst Information Center (a national clearinghouse for information on women and work), a monthly newsletter, and discounts on publications and speaker rates.

Publications: Among Catalyst's child care–related publications are *Resources for Today's Parent, The Corporate Guide to Parental Leaves, Report on a National Study of Parental Leaves, Corporate Child Care Options,* and *Work and Family Seminars: Corporations Respond to Employees' Needs.*

Center for Parent Education
81 Wyman Street
Waban, MA 02168
(617) 964-2442

Description: The Center for Parent Education is a nonprofit public service organization established by Dr. Burton White in 1978. The center's focus is on two major programs: public education through the use of radio, television, books, and magazines, and the provision of support services to professionals in the rapidly growing field of parent education. All services are based on the validity of three fundamental ideas: first, that the educational consequences of the experiences of the first three years of life contribute heavily to lifelong development; second, that lack of assistance and support to the child's first teachers (usually the parents) leads to extra stress, reduced pleasure, and educational losses; and third, that effective programs can be implemented immediately. The center was instrumental in launching the Missouri Parents as Teachers pilot program for 1981–1985.

Publications: The center has produced Dr. White's *The First Three Years of Life,* a television series about learning from birth to age 3, as well as publications from the Harvard Preschool Project and the Center for Parent Education (research reports, policy papers, assessment manuals, and so on). Current and back issues of the *Center for Parent Education Newsletter* are also available.

Center for Effective Services for Children
P.O. Box 27412
Washington, DC 20038-7412
(202) 785-9524

Description: The Center for Effective Services for Children is a newly established not-for-profit organization dedicated to improving the effectiveness and efficiency of children's services. The center works at the federal, state, local, and community levels to help create environments in which comprehensive, community-based, family-focused services can thrive. The center is concerned with the full spectrum of child-serving programs, including child care and early education, child health, foster care, adoption, and child protective systems.

Publications: The center's first major publication, *Building Early Childhood Systems,* is a source of comprehensive and creative ideas on how to transform the current patchwork of programs for young children into a pluralistic and coordinated early childhood system that can better serve the needs of today's families and children.

Child Care Action Campaign (CCAC)
330 Seventh Avenue, 17th Floor
New York, NY 10001
(212) 239-0138

Description: CCAC's mission is to stimulate and support the development of policies and programs that will increase the availability of quality, affordable child care for the benefit of children, their families, and the economic well-being of the United States. CCAC research has drawn from the correlation between the needs of working families and national prosperity. Research findings are made available to the general public as well as government and corporate policymakers. CCAC advocates for additional investment in child care by employers, labor, and federal, state, and local governments.

Membership: Corporate ($250.00), organization ($100.00), and individual ($20.00) membership programs are available.

Publications: In addition to the bimonthly newsletter *Child Care ActioNews,* CCAC publishes up-to-date *Information Guides* on relevant issues. CCAC's research and public policy publications include *Making the Connections: Public-Private Partnerships in Child Care; Building Links: Developer Initiatives for Financing Child Care;* and *Child Care: The Bottom Line.*

Child Care Employee Project (CCEP)
6536 Telegraph Avenue, Suite A-201
Oakland, CA 94609
(510) 653-9889

Description: The Child Care Employee Project is a national resource and advocacy organization dedicated to improving the quality of child care through better wages and working conditions for child care staff. The organization documents trends in the child care work force, advocates for improved public policies that support fair employment practices for child care staff, and provides resource materials. CCEP compiles an annual report on state and local salary surveys.

Membership: Regular membership fees are $25.00 per year ($15.00 for child care workers). Members receive the CCEP newsletter and an annual salary summary.

Publications: CCEP's newsletter, *Child Care Employee News,* is published three times a year. Other reports on research and policy developments aimed at upgrading the child care profession are also available. Of special note is the

National Child Care Staffing Study, a comprehensive profile of people working in child care centers and their relationship to the quality of care children receive.

Child Care Law Center (CCLC)
22 Second Street, 5th Floor
San Francisco, CA 94105
(415) 495-5498

Description: The Child Care Law Center works exclusively to resolve the legal issues that surround the provision of child care. The center works with nonprofit organizations, family day care providers, parents, attorneys, child care policymakers, government and community agencies, and unions and employers. The center's three main service areas are legal consultation, representation, and training; dissemination of information through the Law and Policy Resources Bank; and consultation and technical assistance concerning legislative and regulatory issues.

Membership: Supporters donating $25.00 or more receive the CCLC newsletter and a discount of 15 percent on publications.

Publications: CCLC publishes a newsletter covering the emerging legal issues in child care as well as a series of publications that explain child care-related legal issues in lay terms. Included in the series are reports on liability, insurance, nonprofit incorporation, tax-exempt status, contracts, taxes, child abuse, zoning, building codes, school-age child care, and legal and tax aspects of employer-supported child care.

Child Welfare League of America (CWLA)
440 First Street, NW, Suite 310
Washington, DC 20001-2085
(202) 638-2952

Description: Established in 1920, CWLA is one of the oldest and largest membership organizations serving the needs of children in North America. CWLA sets standards for all child welfare services and works to transfer its ideals into practice through advocacy and training. CWLA concerns itself with national policy on such issues as adoption, foster care, child abuse, day care, runaway youth, and adolescent pregnancy and parenting.

Membership: Full membership is available to public and private agencies providing direct services to children (dues are based on the agency's annual child welfare budget). Supporting advocate membership ($400.00) is available to organizations that do not provide direct services to children (e.g., planning councils, unions, and foundations).

Publications: CWLA publishes a bimonthly journal, *Child Welfare;* a newsletter reporting on the latest program and policy initiatives for children's services,

Children's VOICE; and a biweekly, *Washington Social Legislation Bulletin.* The organization also publishes books and monographs dealing with topics of interest to the child welfare professional.

Children's Defense Fund (CDF)
25 E Street, NW
Washington, DC 20001
(202) 628-8787

Description: Child care is one of several children's issues with which the Children's Defense Fund is concerned. Others include health, education, adolescent pregnancy prevention, child welfare, housing and homelessness, child poverty, and youth employment. CDF's emphasis is on the needs of poor, minority, and disabled children, and the organization's focus is on programs and policies that affect large numbers of children, rather than on helping families on a case-by-case basis. CDF has dedicated a significant portion of its resources to developing and organizing support for comprehensive child care legislation that will make it easier for low-income parents to obtain safe, affordable child care. It was considered a driving force behind the Child Care and Development Block Grant program passed by legislation in 1990. CDF has helped 39 state child care alliances improve child care in their states.

Publications: CDF Reports, the Children's Defense Fund's monthly newsletter, is made available through subscription. Prominent among CDF's other publications is *A Children's Defense Budget,* CDF's annual look at the status of children in America.

Children's Foundation (CF)
725 Fifteenth Street, NW, Suite 505
Washington, DC 20005
(202) 347-3300

Description: The Children's Foundation is a national advocacy organization specializing in the area of child care and child support enforcement. Their work has involved national and local action on issues such as welfare reform, federal food assistance programs for children, health care and housing, affordable high-quality child care, and enforcement of court-ordered child support. Two of CF's current projects are the National Family Day Care Project and the National Child Support Project. Additionally, CF produces training materials for child care providers and antibias multicultural materials for use in the family day care setting.

Publications: Quarterly information bulletins are published for both the Family Day Care and Child Support projects. Various directories, pamphlets, fact sheets, and training materials are also available.

Clearinghouse on Implementation of Child Care and Eldercare Services (CHOICES)
U.S. Department of Labor, Women's Bureau
200 Constitution Avenue, NW
Room 53306
Washington, DC 20210
(202) 523-4486/(800) 827-5335

Description: The Women's Bureau has primary responsibility for the child care issue in the Department of Labor. Charged with the mission of formulating standards and policies that promote the welfare of wage-earning women, the Women's Bureau has established an informational clearinghouse designed to keep employers informed on the latest research and resources available for addressing the critical workplace issue of child care.

Publications: Copies of the Women's Bureau's *Work and Family Resource Kit* and other publications are available upon request.

The Conference Board Work and Family Center
845 Third Avenue
New York, NY 10022-6601
(212) 759-0900

Description: The Conference Board is a management information service, the purpose of which is to assist senior executives and other leaders in arriving at sound decisions on critical issues of corporate policy, management practice, economics, and public policy. As part of the Conference Board's Human Resources Program Group, the Work and Family Center is a national clearinghouse of information designed to assist the business community in responding to changes in work and family relationships. The center is concerned with how modern families are affected by what happens in the workplace and how the workplace is influenced by the special needs and resources that family members bring to their jobs.

Publications: Research studies are issued as Conference Board reports, research bulletins, or other periodic monographs, and are distributed to Conference Board associates and other interested organizations.

Council for Early Childhood Professional Recognition (CDA)
1718 Connecticut Avenue, NW, Suite 500
Washington, DC 20009
(202) 265-9090/(800) 424-4310

Description: Initially formed in the early 1970s as a collaborative effort between the early childhood profession and the Administration for Children, Youth and Families (ACYF), the CDA Program created a new category of early childhood professional—the child development associate. The CDA Program maintains two separate branches. One is designed to promote a variety of training experiences for early childhood staff and family child care providers. To date, nearly 40,000 CDA credentials have been awarded to individuals who have successfully completed the necessary requirements. The other branch is designed to establish national standards for the evaluation and credentialing of competent child care staff. Child care regulations in 49 states and the District of Columbia list the CDA credential as a qualification for teaching staff and/or directors (only Indiana does not currently include CDA in its licensing requirements).

Publications: Various public awareness publications are available regarding the CDA credentialing process. *Competence,* CDA's quarterly newsletter, is also available.

Families and Work Institute
330 Seventh Avenue
New York, NY 10001
(212) 465-2044

Description: The Families and Work Institute is a nonprofit research and planning organization committed to developing new approaches for balancing the changing needs of America's families with the continuing need for workplace productivity. The institute conducts policy research on a broad range of issues related to the changing demographics of the work force and operates a national clearinghouse on work and family life. It serves decision makers from all sectors of society—business, education, community, and government. The institute conducts four major activities: research, dissemination, strategic planning, and management training.

Publications: Recently published reports include *The Corporate Reference Guide, The State Reference Guide,* and *Education Before School: Investing in Quality Child Care.*

Family Resource Coalition
200 South Michigan, Suite 1520
Chicago, IL 60604-2404
(312) 341-0900

Description: The coalition is a national not-for-profit membership organization that represents some 2,500 professionals who work with family resource programs and issues across the United States and Canada. Its major function is to provide information, technical assistance, and training for people involved in providing preventive, community-based resources for families.

Membership: Individual membership is $30 per year, agency/organizational membership is $60.

Publications: Program Builders Package includes the following resources: *Programs To Strengthen Families: A Resource Guide; The Family Resource Program Builder: Blueprints for Designing and Operating Programs for Parents;* and *Building Strong Foundations: Evaluation Strategies for Family Resource Programs.*

Head Start Bureau
P.O. Box 1182
Washington, DC 20013
(202) 245-0572

Description: Head Start was launched by the federal government in 1965 to help young children from low-income families get a better start in life. Head Start was designed to provide a full program of educational, health, nutrition, and social services to 3–5-year-olds. Approximately 16 percent of the preschool children now living in poverty in this country participate in Head Start programs. One important concept of Head Start is its emphasis on involving parents in all phases of the program.

Publications: None.

High/Scope Educational Research Foundation
600 North River Street
Ypsilanti, MI 48198
(313) 485-2000

Description: The High/Scope Foundation is an independent nonprofit organization formally established in 1970 by Dr. David Weikart. High/Scope's work centers on research, curriculum development, professional training, and public policy advocacy on the learning and development of children from infancy through adolescence, with a special emphasis on the early years. High/Scope is known for its continuing research on the long-term effects of preschool education on children living in poverty. The foundation is currently engaged in a national and worldwide study that explores patterns of early childhood education and care.

Publications: High/Scope Press publishes research reports, policy papers, and a wide range of curriculum materials. High/Scope periodicals include a quarterly magazine, *High Scope Resource,* and a bimonthly newsletter, *Extensions.*

National Association for the Education of Young Children (NAEYC)
1834 Connecticut Avenue, NW
Washington, DC 20009-5786
(202) 232-8777/(800) 424-2460

Description: NAEYC, a nonprofit professional organization of nearly 75,000 members, is dedicated to improving the quality of care and education provided for young children (birth through 8 years) and their families. The organization hosts the largest educational conference in the country. NAEYC also administers the National Academy of Early Childhood Programs (CDA), a voluntary national accreditation system for high-quality early childhood programs. The NAEYC Information Service was established to offer access to extensive early childhood-related information. The Public Affairs Division provides policy-related information and legislative analysis. NAEYC's primary goals of improving the professional practice of early childhood education and building public support for high-quality early childhood programs are shared and implemented by a national network of more than 400 affiliate groups.

Membership: Regular and comprehensive memberships are available.

Publications: In addition to the bimonthly journal *Young Children,* NAEYC publishes an extensive array of brochures, books, videos, and posters.

National Association of Child Care Resource and Referral Agencies (NACCRRA)
2116 Campus Drive SE
Rochester, MN 53904
(507) 287-2220/(800) 462-1660

Description: NACCRRA is an association of agencies (public and private) in all 50 states whose function is the delivery of child care referral services in their local communities. NACCRRA's purpose is to promote the development, maintenance, and expansion of quality child care resource and referral. The association sponsors annual regional and national conferences, provides technical assistance and training for agencies and referral counselors, maintains a clearinghouse of information, implements standard-setting policies, and publishes an association newsletter.

Membership: Voting memberships are open to resource and referral agencies. Auxiliary memberships are open to any individual or organization who supports the goals of NACCRRA.

Publications: NACCRRA has collaborated on *The Complete Guide to Choosing Child Care,* a book for parents and professionals. The NACCRRA newsletter, *CCR&R Issues,* is included with membership or as a separate subscription for $25.00.

National Association of Family Day Care (NAFDC)
725 Fifteenth Street, NW, Suite 505
Washington, DC 20005
(202) 347-3356

Description: NAFDC represents a support network of some 200,000 family child care providers, local and state associations, child care food programs, and resource and referral organizations. NAFDC works to increase public awareness of the licensed family child care option and promotes professional growth and networking opportunities among its members. NAFDC's National Family Day Care Accreditation Program offers professional recognition to those providers who have been assessed to offer a quality of care that goes beyond minimum standards regulated by each state. NAFDC also hosts a national Family Day Care Conference annually.

Membership: Individual, association, and agency membership options are available.

Publications: In collaboration with the Children's Foundation, *NAFDC publishes the National Directory of Associations and Support Groups* and a bi-monthly newsletter, *The New National Perspective.*

National Association of Hospital-Affiliated Child Care Programs (NAHACCP)
Parkside Children's Services
Lutheran General Health Care System
9375 Church Street
Des Plaines, IL 60016
(708) 824-5180

Description: The NAHACCP serves as a network to more than half of the hospital-sponsored child care programs in the country. It provides information, support, and a national network of expertise to hospitals and other corporations interested in establishing child care services.

Membership: NAHACCP membership is open to all individuals or organizations operating hospital-affiliated child care programs, interested in starting programs at health care facilities, or supporting these programs.

Publications: NAHACCP publishes a member newsletter and a national directory of colleagues and programs.

National Center for Clinical Infant Programs (NCCIP)
2000 14th Street North, Suite 380
Arlington, VA 22201-2500
(703) 528-4300

Description: The work of the center is based on the premise that the care that every child receives during infancy can have a critical impact on future functioning; the center works toward developing integrated approaches to research and providing a forum for the exchange of information emanating from clinical infant and early childhood research. The center offers a fellowship program, a biennial national training institute and regional institutes and workshops, and a clearinghouse of information relating to infant health, mental health, and development.

Publications: A bulletin, *Zero to Three,* issued five times per year; a book-length series called *Clinical Infant Reports;* and a series of papers that are used to incorporate scientific knowledge about infants into public policy and planning. A task force has been designated to research and report on the effects of infant child care.

National Child Care Association (NCCA)
1029 Railroad Street
Conyers (Atlanta), GA 30207
(800) 543-7161

Description: Formed in 1988, NCCA represents member proprietary child care centers in legislative, public awareness, and educational matters. With a primary mission of protecting the interests of licensed, proprietary providers of child care services, the organization also sponsors annual training and exhibition conferences and maintains a referral system for member centers. Along with the national headquarters, 19 state affiliates have been formed, in Alabama, Arizona, California, Colorado, Florida, Georgia, Illinois, Kentucky, Louisiana, Maryland, Mississippi, Montana, Nevada, New Jersey, New York, Oklahoma, South Carolina, Texas, and Virginia. Through grant funding from Hardee's Foods Systems, NCCA has been instrumental in establishing two organizations that complement NCCA goals: the American Association of Early Childhood Educators (AAECE), a teacher/caregiver association designed to provide benefits and to lead in the professional development of center staff, and the National Childcare Parents Association, an organization concerned with informing and involving parents in the development of child care policy.

Membership: Regular membership is limited to licensed private child care centers.

Publications: NCAA publishes a quarterly newsletter, *National Focus.*

National Coalition for Campus Child Care
Southern Illinois University at Edwardsville
Early Childhood Center
Edwardsville, IL 62026
(618) 692-2000, ext. 2556

Description: This coalition serves as a vehicle for sharing information among those who are involved and interested in providing campus-based child care. Services include support for the establishment, maintenance, and, where appropriate, expansion of campus child care programs and support for the individuals involved in the provision of campus child care.

Among the coalition's activities are a yearly national conference, a semiannual newsletter, a national network of campus child care programs, a packet of materials on starting a campus child care program, and consultation services.

Membership: Membership is available to individuals ($35.00), organizations ($90.00), and students ($15.00). Members receive three newsletters, a membership list, and an updated bibliography yearly, policy and strategy papers, and reduced rates for conferences and publications.

Publications: Publications available to both members and nonmembers include *A Collection of Campus Child Care Needs Assessments, A Collection of Campus Building Plans,* and *National Campus Child Care Study 1989.*

National Council of Jewish Women (NCJW) Center for the Child
53 West Twenty-third Street
6th Floor
New York, NY 10010
(212) 645-4048

Description: NCJW Center for the Child is a research institute designed to increase public awareness and understanding of children's issues, to improve programs for children, with special emphasis on prevention, and to influence both public and private policy affecting the welfare of children and their families. Mothers in the Workplace, an NCJW project, is a national study of how working parents reconcile the often conflicting demands of job and family life. Field research was conducted in more than 100 communities across the country. Under a grant from the Women's Bureau of the U.S. Department of Labor, NCJW launched the Work/Family Project, a four-stage program to promote employer support for child care. The project is designed to include information collected from employers and child care providers, community needs assessment, conferences and seminars for employers, and community awareness and education campaigns.

Publications: In 1972, NCJW published a report on a national survey of family child care titled *Windows on Day Care.* Various reports and a marketing kit for family child care providers are also available.

Parent Action
2 Hopkins Plaza
Suite 2100
Baltimore, MD 21201
(410) 752-1790

Description: Parent Action is a national membership organization dedicated to empowering parents to speak out for what they need to do their jobs as parents. The organization advocates on behalf of parents on family issues such as tax policies, health care, child care, and employment regulations. Parent Action is dedicated to working with parents to make the United States "family-friendly."

Membership: Suggested membership contribution is $25.00 per family.

Publications: Parent Action publishes a quarterly newsletter and sends regular issue updates to members.

Save the Children/Child Care Support Center
1447 Peachtree Street, NE
Suite 700
Atlanta, GA 30309
(404) 885-1578

Description: Save the Children, founded in 1932, is an international voluntary organization dedicated to improving the economic and social well-being of poor children. The mission of Save the Children is to help effect lasting, positive changes in the lives of disadvantaged children. In all its activities, Save the Children works with communities, teaching self-help skills and providing programs and direct services to help improve the lives of children. The Save the Children/Child Care Support Center has a special mission to improve the lives of children in child care. This includes working to improve the quality, availability, and affordability of child care services in the metropolitan Atlanta area and in other areas of Georgia. As part of the organization's national focus on child care, it works with both rural and urban communities, offering assistance in developing and implementing programs to help improve the quality of child care. The center shares information through individual consultation, publications, conferences, and workshops. It also sponsors an annual Family Day Care Technical Assistance Conference each spring.

Publications: Staff members have written publications on the design and operation of programs, child care policy, family child care, child care administration, and other topics. Some publications were originally written for use in Georgia, but could be adapted for use in other areas of the country.

School-Age Child Care Project (SACC Project)
Wellesley College
Center for Research on Women
Wellesley, MA 02181-8259
(617) 283-2500

Description: The School-Age Child Care Project was initiated in 1979 in response to the expressed needs of parents, school administrators, child care providers, and local and state policymakers for information and assistance in understanding the "latchkey kids" problem and in developing options for services and policies. Since its inception, the SACC Project has helped shape many government initiatives on before- and after-school child care through its research and other policy-related work. The project conducts research, designs workshops and conferences, develops publications and videotapes, and provides technical assistance and consultation, with the dual aim of expanding the supply and improving the quality of child care for school-age children across the United States.

Publications: The SACC Project's Action Research Papers are a series of reports on topics of importance to the field, such as the role of city governments in school-age child care, the use of television in school-age child care, and the changing role of libraries in the out-of-school lives of children. The project also publishes training manuals that describe how to start a school-age child care program, how to work with parents of school-age children, and how to use an intergenerational approach in developing school-age child care programs.

The Urban Institute
2100 M Street, NW
Washington, DC 20037
(202) 833-7200

Description: The Urban Institute is a nonprofit organization that conducts research on policy-related social issues, including but not limited to child care issues. Recent child care-related projects of the institute have included studies on the child care arrangements of American children and the characteristics of child care providers in the United States. These reports are based on data collected in late 1989 and early 1990 on large, uniformly representative samples of children and providers.

Publications: The quarterly newsletter *The Urban Institute: Policy and Research Report* includes current information on child care. Copies of child care research findings are available in the publications *A Profile of Child Care Settings* and *The National Child Care Survey.*

Wheelock College Center for Child Care Policy and Training
200 The Riverway
Boston, MA 02215
(617) 734-5200, ext. 211

Description: A newly established extension of Wheelock College's long-standing mission of improving the quality of life for children and families, the Center for Child Care Policy and Training addresses issues in the areas of professional development and policy for all program types in the field of early childhood care and education. Current center projects include compiling information on current state policies affecting professional development; working with state and community-based groups to de elop innovative projects; networking with other national early childhood care and education groups to influence policy, program, and funding strategies in the area of career development; offering advanced seminars in child care administration at local sites throughout the United States; and serving as a clearinghouse for information on the development of state policies.

Publications: The center publishes the *State of the States* report—a compilation of information on state licensing standards, funding of training in the early childhood field, teacher certification programs, training sites, and emerging initiatives.

Windflower Enterprises, Inc.
142 South Claremont Street
Colorado Springs, CO 80910

Description: Windflower is a partnership of child care professionals that provides child care training to center and home-based providers and parenting skill training for parents of young children. The organization has developed Second Helping, a 32-hour advanced enrichment training program for family child care professionals. In addition, Windflower is actively involved in advocacy efforts to put self-determination of the child care industry in the hands of those who provide care for children.

Publications: The Provider Connection: A Closer Look at the Relationship between Family Child Care Providers, Resource and Referrals, and Other Child Care Agencies is a Windflower position paper that discusses the difficult issues that exist between providers and support agencies.

Work/Family Directions (W/FD)
930 Commonwealth Avenue South
Boston, MA 02215
(800) 346-1535

Description: Work/Family Directions was established in 1984 to purchase child care resource and referral services for the employees of IBM in more than 200 communities nationwide. It has grown to become the largest provider of corporate resource and referral services in the country, subcontracting with a network of approximately 300 community-based resource and referral agencies on behalf of a wide base of national multisite corporations. Other corporate services available through W/FD include research and strategic labor force planning services, education and training programs, and informational resources. Another aspect of W/FD's child care support function is to assist in the development of new family child care homes and centers in communities servicing corporate clients. Work/Family Directions also has a division that is responsible for developing elder care solutions for corporate clients.

Publications: Parent support materials include Questions Working Parents Ask, I Can Take Care of Myself, In-Home Child Care, The Child Care Handbook, and

Not Enough Child Care. Employer/advocate resources include *A Little Bit under the Weather: A Look at Care for Mildly Ill Children and Achieving Balance.* Resource and referral support materials include *Publicity Materials for Family Day Care Recruiting* and *Family Day Care: Meeting Recruitment Challenges.*

Yale University
Bush Center on Child Development and Social Policy
P.O. Box 11A
Yale Station
New Haven, CT 06520
(203) 432-4575

Description: The Bush Center focuses on "research, training and public information to support the creation of sound public policy to improve the lives of America's children and families." Under the direction of Edward Zigler, the center originated the School of the 21st Century program, which incorporates comprehensive family services into the public schools. Child care components include school-based, year-round, all-day care for children ages 3–5, school-based before- and after-school and vacation care for children ages 5–12, and support and training for family day care providers in the school's neighborhood. The program is currently operating in various forms in Colorado, Missouri, Connecticut, and Wyoming. The Bush Center offers technical assistance to school districts and to city and state governments that wish to integrate a child care component into the public school system.

Publications: The concept of the School of the 21st Century is detailed in *Child Care Choices: Balancing the Needs of Children, Families, and Society,* by Edward Zigler and Mary E. Lang. Dr. Zigler has also authored *The Parental Leave Crisis: Toward a National Policy.*

5

Reference Materials

Books

Adams, Gina. **Who Knows How Safe? The Status of State Efforts To Ensure Quality Child Care.** Washington, DC: Children's Defense Fund, 1990. 140p. $5.95. ISBN 0-938008-82-X.

This book analyzes each state's child care regulatory policies in terms of standards, monitoring, and enforcement. It includes several charts that allow for at-a-glance comparisons among states. Unfortunately, its findings include the conclusion that states do not provide even minimal protections for nearly half of all children who are cared for outside their homes.

Adolf, Barbara, and Karol Rose. **The Employer's Guide to Child Care.** Westport, CT: Praeger, 1988. 202p. $37.95. ISBN 0-275-92892-8.

This handbook uses research results and practical planning guidelines for employer-supported child care as well as specific illustrations of recent developments in the field. Both indirect and direct types of child care support are explained, with frank discussion outlining the pros and cons of each type.

Auerbach, Judith D. **In the Business of Child Care: Employer Initiatives and Working Women.** Westport, CT: Praeger, 1988. 183p. $39.95. ISBN 0-275-92858-6.

Exploring child care from a sociological viewpoint is the heart of Auerbach's research. She argues that "the current lack of child care services in the United

States reflects the strength of ideological resistance to and political confusion about the role of extrafamilial child care." She believes this resistance stems from the deep-rooted belief that "nurturance is woman's work, that it is not something that should be compensated, and that government should not intervene in the private lives of families and family members." In this context, Auerbach traces the history of child care and explores the role of employer initiatives as a means of responsibly resolving child care needs.

Beardsley, Lyda. **Good Day/Bad Day: The Child's Experience of Child Care.** New York: Teachers College Press, 1990. 176p. $15.95. ISBN 0-8077-3039-4.

This book examines the issue of quality child care from the child's perspective. The author introduces a group of representative preschool-age children and contrasts their experiences through a hypothetical day in each of two very different child care situations. Although fictional, the characters and incidents described are based on real observations of children and teachers in poor- and good-quality child care environments. The events and interactions described are interpreted for the reader in annotated sections that provide references to current research regarding each area discussed.

Berezin, Judith. **The Complete Guide to Choosing Child Care.** New York: Random House, 1990. 258p. $12.95. ISBN 0-679-73100-8.

A collaborative effort of New York City's Child Care Inc. and the National Association of Child Care Resource and Referral Agencies, this book discusses child care options, children's developmental needs, and child care advocacy. Its appendix includes child care resources and a comprehensive listing of community-based and state resource and referral agencies.

Burud, Sandra L., Pamela R. Aschbacher, and Jacquelyn McCroskey. **Employer-Supported Child Care: Investing in Human Resources.** Dover, MA: Auburn House, 1984. 352p. $16.95. ISBN 0-86569-122-3.

Based on a study conducted by the National Employer-Supported Child Care Project, this book provides insight into how employers initiate and establish child care support programs. The book is divided into five sections dedicated to the following topic areas: overview, benefits to companies, determining needs and decision making, implementing program options, and guidelines and support materials. Field tested how-to materials include a comprehensive needs assessment.

Cahan, Emily D. **Past Caring: A History of U.S. Preschool Care and Education for the Poor (1820–1965).** New York: Columbia University Press, 1989. 59p. $5.95. ISBN 0-926582-00-3.

The two-tiered system of child care is traced back to the nineteenth and early twentieth centuries in this historical review. It contrasts the system of custodial group child care for low-income families with the preschool education system available to families able to afford it.

Child Care Action Campaign. **Making the Connections: Public-Private Partnerships in Child Care.** New York: 1991. 56p. $10.00 (members); $20.00 (nonmembers). No ISBN.

Child Care Action Campaign's Advisory Panel consists of 525 private and public sector leaders from across the nation. This report examines the funding, design, and status of innovative partnerships among private businesses, voluntary organizations, and public agencies.

Children's Defense Fund. **The State of America's Children.** Washington, DC: 1991 (updated annually). 170p. $13.95. ISBN 0-938008-86-2.

The ten lessons to help us through the 1990s that Children's Defense Fund president Marian Wright Edelman lists in the introduction make this year's volume worth reading. However, the research and data on CDF's focus issues—family income and employment, child care, health, education, youth development, housing and homelessness, and vulnerable children—make this an indispensable source of information for child care advocates.

Child Care Employee Project. **Who Cares? Child Care Teachers and the Quality of Care in America.** Oakland, CA: 1989. 20p. $10.00 (executive summary). No ISBN.

This report of the National Child Care Staffing Study looks at how early childhood teachers and their working conditions affect the quality of center-based child care in the United States. Chief among several significant findings is that "good quality care requires an environment that values adults as well as children." Poor working conditions and low wages are the predominant causes of the high incidence of staff turnover in child care centers.

Fernandez, John P. **The Politics and Reality of Family Care in Corporate America.** Lexington, MA: Lexington Books, 1990. 276p. $18.95. ISBN 0-669-21562-7.

After surveying more than 26,000 employees in 30 companies employing between 50 and 15,000 people, Fernandez concludes that company policies have not kept pace with the changing labor force and changes in the demographics of the American family. He presents family care as a corporate competitive issue that benefits the corporate bottom line through increased productivity. The appendix includes a comprehensive description and list of corresponding advantages and disadvantages for many types of family care solutions.

Flating, Sonja. **Child Care: A Parent's Guide.** New York: Facts on File, 1991. 173p. $24.95. ISBN 0-8160-2232-1.

Written from a parent's perspective, this book attempts to address some of the concerns parents have about child care, such as: What should you look for in a child care provider? How can parents fit child care into a tight family budget? Are there advantages/disadvantages of large versus small day-care centers? What are the alternatives to traditional child care? How can parents overcome the guilt they often feel when they leave children with a provider or at a day care center? What can workers do to convince their employers to offer on-site care?

Galinsky, Ellen, and Dana Friedman. **The Corporate Reference Guide to Work-Family Programs.** New York: Families and Work Institute, 1991. 437 p. $149.00. No ISBN.

This is an extensive reference volume on work-family issues that contains case studies of top-ranking family-friendly companies, the typical states of development of corporate work-family programs, mini-case studies on a range of work-family options, and a comparative analysis of family-supportive policies in 188 companies across 30 industries. It introduces the FWI Family Friendly Index, a yardstick by which companies can assess their own programs and policies.

Hayes, Cheryl D., John L. Palmer, and Martha J. Zaslow, eds. **Who Cares for America's Children?** Washington, DC: National Academy Press, 1990. 362p. $24.95. ISBN 0-309-04032-9.

Resulting from a two-year study of child care programs and policies, this book examines the costs, effects, and feasibility of alternative child care services. The authors examine the "trilemma" of child care—affordability, accessibility, and quality—particularly as it relates to low- and moderate-income families. The need for national child care standards and mandated protected family leave policies is also stressed.

Howes, Carolle. **Keeping Current in Child Care Research.** Washington, DC: National Association for the Education of Young Children, 1986 (with annual updates). 280p. $20.00. ISBN 0-935989-01-3.

This annually updated binder presents concise information describing recent child care research. Separate sections report on findings related to attachment, social development, cognitive development, effects of child care, indicators of quality, and the stability of child care situations.

Kagan, Sharon L. **United We Stand: Collaboration for Child Care and Early Education Services.** New York: Teachers College Press, 1991. 168p. $23.95. ISBN 0-8077-3135-8.

This volume is about the process of forming partnerships and integrating services that coordinate and collaborate on behalf of children. It illustrates the interrelatedness of early child care and education and the human services delivery system in the United States. It provides practical and theoretical information on ways to improve service delivery to both mainstream and special population groups of young children.

Kammerman, Sheila B., Alfred J. Kahn, and Paul Kingston. **Maternity Policies and Working Women.** New York: Columbia University Press, 1985. 180p. $17.00. ISBN 0-231-05751-2.

This team of researchers looks at the present status of maternity benefits in this country and gives an analysis of the relationship of those benefits to sex discrimination, civil rights, and the women's movement. The authors examine innovative approaches being offered by individual companies and explore the need for comprehensive social policies and appropriate legislation that provide job protection and leave benefits for maternity-related purposes.

Kahn, Alfred, and Sheila Kammerman. **Child Care: Facing the Hard Choices.** Dover, MA: Auburn House, 1987. 273p. $26.00. ISBN 0-86569-164-9.

The authors, both respected researchers, examine child care policy options and programs in this volume. Among the options they discuss are information and referral services, vendor/voucher programs, state actions, public school child care, employer-sponsored child care, and family day care.

Kisker, Ellen Eliason, Sandra Hofferth, Deborah Phillips, and Elizabeth Farquhar. **National Child Care Survey.** Washington, DC: U.S. Department of Education, 1991. 2 vols. 492 p. $48.00 Hardcover ISBN 0-87766-504-4. $23.50. Paperback ISBN 0-87766-505-2.

This report provides comprehensive and recent information on the operation, supply, and use of licensed and regulated child care centers and family day care homes. The report examines sponsorship, admissions, enrollment, staffing patterns and turnover, program goals and activities, program structure, and fees, as well as trends that have developed since the last national study was completed in 1976. The study was conducted in a nationally representative sample of U.S. counties. Interviews were held with about 2,600 providers, including directors of church-based programs, part-day preschools, school-based programs, Head Start, nonprofit and for-profit centers, and regulated home-based providers. This report was closely coordinated with the National Child Care Survey 1990, a household survey of parents with young children sponsored by the Administration for

Children, Youth and Families, U.S. Department of Health and Human Services, and the National Association for the Education of Young Children. The Demand and Supply of Child Care in 1990, available from NAEYC, summarizes the highlights from both studies.

Linder, Eileen W., Mary C. Mattis, and June R. Rogers. **When Churches Mind the Children.** Ypsilanti, MI: High/Scope Press, 1983. 176p. $10.00. ISBN 0-931114-23-3.

Churches and synagogues constitute one of the nation's largest providers of child care. The authors of this volume cite and interpret findings from an extensive study done by the Child Day Care Project of the National Council of Churches of Christ. The study examined various forms of church-based care, goals and policies, fees and funding sources, clientele, and specific insight from church center directors.

Morgan, Gwen. **The National State of Child Care Regulation.** Washington, DC: National Association for the Education of Young Children, 1991. $25.00. ISBN 0-9618201-0-1.

This is an updated report covering state licensing system information on such topics as the types of child care programs regulated, state-designated licensing agencies, methods of monitoring, and enforcement. Key requirements are highlighted, including staff qualifications, ratios, group size, discipline, parental role, the development aspects of the program, immunizations and other key health requirements, physical space requirements, and criminal records checks.

Nelson, Margaret K. **Negotiated Care: The Experience of Family Day Care Providers.** Philadelphia: Temple University Press, 1991. 305p. $34.95. ISBN 0-87722-728-4.

This volume in Temple University Press's Women in the Political Economy series explores the daily lives of family child care providers. Basing her findings upon numerous interviews, surveys, recent feminist literature, and investigations of women's involvement in home-based work, Nelson presents the dilemmas providers face in their relationships with parents, with their own families, with state regulatory representatives, and with the children they care for. She links these dilemmas to the paradoxical relationship between public reality and public policy—while the demand for inexpensive, informal child care services constantly increases, public policy supplies only limited resources and support along with a surplus of scrutiny.

Phillips, Deborah, ed. **Quality in Child Care: What Does Research Tell Us?** Washington, DC: National Association for the Education of Young Children, 1987. 127p. $6.00. ISBN 0-935989-08-0.

The findings of five researchers are incorporated into this monograph exploring indicators of child care quality. Studies include an analysis of identifiable components of good-quality child care, a comparison of the qualitative features of various forms of child care (e.g., family child care, center-based care, in-home care), the integral effect of child care experiences and family background, and the distinction between indicators of quality that can be regulated and those that cannot.

Platt, Elizabeth Balliett. **Scenes from Day Care: How Teachers Teach and What Children Learn.** New York: Teachers College Press, 1992. 128p. $16.95. ISBN 0-8077-3131-5.

This book records in detail the small events that happen every day in child care. Through a minute examination of what actually happens to children in specific situations, positives and negatives of the child care experience are identified.

Reisman, Barbara, Amy Moore, and Karen Fitzgerald. **Child Care: The Bottom Line: An Economic and Child Care Policy Paper.** New York: Child Care Action Campaign, 1988. 91p. $20.00. No ISBN.

This policy paper outlines the benefits of more and better child care options for the federal government, individual states, employers, and families. Suggested policy changes are outlined as a means to achieve a child care delivery system that meets the needs of both families and the U.S. economy.

Zigler, Edward F., and Edmund W. Gordon, eds. **Day Care: Scientific and Social Policy Issues.** Dover, MA: Auburn House, 1981. 515p. $16.95. ISBN 0-86569-109-6.

Produced under the authority of the American Orthopsychiatric Association, this volume combines research on the effects of day care with policy analyses on the delivery of day care. Included are a five-year follow-up of participants in the Yale Child Welfare Research Program and other important research findings.

Zigler, Edward F., and Mary E. Lang. **Child Care Choices: Balancing the Needs of Children, Families and Society.** New York: Macmillan, 1991. 271p. $22.95. ISBN 0-02-935821-2.

Looking at both the successful and the unsuccessful approaches to child care that have been implemented since colonial times in America, the authors present a comprehensive strategy that recognizes the responsibility of government, business, and families to work together in ensuring that all children receive adequate care. The concept of the School of the 21st Century is introduced as a flexible and viable option for providing child care that supports various types of family choices.

Zinser, Caroline. **Raised in East Urban.** New York: Teachers College Press, 1991. 200p. $17.95. ISBN 0-8077-3139-0.

In a unique ethnographic study, Zinser reveals the results of her research in one community in a small northeastern city, showing how child care choices are grounded in the changing economic circumstances of parents who struggle to balance work and family. Using the parents' own words, the author provides insight into the decisions and motivations of parents, child care providers, social workers, and day care administrators.

Newsletters and Periodicals

Child Care ActioNews
Child Care Action Campaign
330 Seventh Avenue, 17th Floor
New York, NY 10001
(212) 239-0138

This is a bimonthly newsletter that includes updates on issues and innovations in child care, with a focus on working parents and the varied spheres of service delivery (public, private, employer sponsored, family child care, center-based care, and so on). *Subscriptions:* individual, $20.00; organizations, $100.00; corporations, $250.00.

Child Care Information Exchange
P.O. Box 2890
Redmond, WA 98073-9977
(206) 883-9394

This bimonthly magazine is aimed at child care center directors and owners. It includes articles related to both the child development and administrative sides of running a center. *Subscriptions:* $35.00 per year, with reduced rates for multiple-year subscriptions.

Day Care Information Service
United Communications Group
4550 Montgomery Avenue, Suite 700
Bethesda, MD 20814-3382
(800) 223-9335

This biweekly newsletter is directed at those with a professional interest in child care. It covers policies on child care, Head Start, early intervention, and preschool. *Subscriptions:* $184.00 per year.

Family Day Caring
Redleaf Press
450 North Syndicate, Suite 5
Saint Paul, MN 55104-4125
(800) 423-8309

This is a bimonthly magazine that covers the national scope of family day care with articles about health and safety, tax and business aspects, activities and ideas, developmental needs of children, and profiles of providers and national projects. *Subscriptions:* $14.95 per year.

Legal Update
Child Care Law Center
22 Second Street, 5th Floor
San Francisco, CA 94105
(415) 495-5498

This newsletter covers current legal issues for legal services organizations, resource and referral agencies, and others interested in the emerging legal issues in child care.

National Report on Work and Family
Bureau of National Affairs
1231 25th Street, NW
Washington, DC 20037
(800) 372-1033

This is a biweekly newsletter that reports on the latest news, regulations, court cases, contract provisions, trends, and programs affecting work and family. *Subscriptions:* $475.00 per year.

The New National Perspective
National Association for Family Day Care
725 Fifteenth Street, NW, Suite 505
Washington, DC 20005
(202) 347-3356

Written by and for family child care providers, this bimonthly publication monitors developments pertaining to running a home-based child care business and promotes quality standards. *Subscriptions:* Included in NAFDC membership.

Work and Family Life
Bank Street College
610 West 112th Street
New York, NY 10025
(212) 875-4651

This monthly newsletter offers advice to parents in dealing with the challenges of child care, time management, caring for elderly relatives, and finding sources of help for family crises. Although individual subscriptions are available, this publication is most widely distributed to employees through employers. Current subscribers include large corporations, small- and medium-sized businesses, nonprofit organizations, government agencies, and health care facilities. *Subscriptions:* $36 per year for individuals; multiple-copy discounts to employers.

Sources of Current Research

For updated reports on research and trends in child care, consult the publications lists of the following organizations:

Bureau of National Affairs
1231 Twenty-fifth Street, NW
Washington, DC 20037
(800) 372-1033

The BNA Special Report Series on Work and Family includes a wide selection of 32-page reports exploring the issues surrounding the work-family relationship. Topics covered include innovative work arrangements, public-private partnerships, training, options in child care and elder care, and new developments in legislation, court decisions, and administrative action. BNA's *Work and Family: The Complete Resource Guide* is a 600-page reference volume that provides comprehensive background information and current details on relevant services, studies and reports, progressive corporate policies, state and federal laws, and pending legislation.

Children's Defense Fund
25 E Street, NW
Washington, DC 20001
(202) 628-8787

The Children's Defense Fund publishes annual updates on the status of America's children in the key areas of family income and employment, child care, health, education, youth development, and housing and homelessness. The organization also provides information on current legislation and newly implemented social policy affecting families.

CHOICES
U.S. Department of Labor, Women's Bureau
200 Constitution Avenue, NW
Room 53306
Washington, DC 20210
(202)523-4486/(800) 827-5335

This clearinghouse provides employers with information to help them implement family-responsive workplace practices. The database offers information, references, examples, and technical assistance on employer-sponsored options that can help workers manage their family responsibilities.

Early Childhood Research Quarterly
Ablex Publishing Corporation
355 Chestnut Street
Norwood, NJ 07648

This quarterly journal, edited by Lillian G. Katz, is an important resource for scholars, researchers, decision makers, and practitioners with an interest in young children from birth to age 8. The publication is jointly sponsored by the National Association for the Education of Young Children and ERIC/EECE.

National Association for the Education of Young Children
1834 Connecticut Avenue, NW
Washington, DC 20009-5786
(800) 424-2460

Along with developmentally appropriate curriculum and teaching resources, NAEYC publishes a series of monographs, reports, and studies related to early childhood, families, public policy, and advocacy.

6

Nonprint Resources

Films and Videocassettes

Child Care Alternatives
Type: Video
Length: 14 minutes
Date: 1990
Cost: $39.00
Source: Meridian Education Corporation
        236 East Front Street
        Bloomington, IL 61701
        (309) 827-5455

Geared to junior and senior high school parent education classes, this video presents an overview of five common forms of nonparental child care situations: the informal arrangement with other family members or friends, licensed in-home care, child care centers, employer-sponsored child care, and government-supported child care.

Child Care Choices
Type: Video (Beta, VHS), 3/4" film
Length: 14 minutes
Date: 1985
Cost: $255.00
Source: Perennial Education, Inc.
        930 Pitner Avenue
        Evanston, IL 60202
        (800) 323-9084

This film discuss current child care options, factors to consider when choosing a child care facility, and suggestions on how to monitor the quality of care children receive.

Child Care Choices: Indoor Safety

Type:	Video
Length:	54 minutes
Date:	1991
Cost:	$279.00
Source:	Bergwall Productions
	106 Charles Lindberg Boulevard
	Uniondale, NY 11553
	(516) 222-1111

This three-video tutorial for child care workers discusses ways to ensure the safety of young children. The three programs—"Making It Safe," "Keeping It Safe," and "Playing It Safe"—incorporate the use of appropriate role models and quality environments for children. A study guide is also available.

Child Day Care in Three Cultures

Type:	*Video (VHS)*
Length:	50 minutes
Date:	1978
Cost:	$325.00
Source:	Campus Film Distributors
	24 Depot Square
	Tuckahoe, NY 10707
	(914) 961-1900

This film provides a cross-cultural comparison of child care programs in Austria, China, and Philadelphia.

Day Care in America: A Study in Progress

Type:	Video (Beta, VHS), 3/4" film
Length:	15 minutes
Date:	c. 1978
Cost:	$75.00
Source:	Walter J. Klein Ltd.
	P.O. Box 2087
	Charlotte, NC 28211
	(704) 542-1403

This film examines how well the nation's child care centers measure up to the increasing need for quality child care.

Day Care Today

Type: Video (Beta, VHS), 3/4" film
Length: 25 minutes
Date: 1972
Cost: $100.00
Source: Polymorph Films
              118 South Street
              Boston, MA 02111
              (800) 223-5107

This program profiles three popular forms of child care centers: an employer-sponsored on-site center, a university-based center, and a community-based infant care center.

Families in the Balance

Type: Video
Length: 23 minutes
Date: 1989
Cost: $36.00
Source: Cornell University
              Audio Visual Center
              8 Research Park
              Ithaca, NY 14850
              (607) 255-2091

In this video, narrated by actress Ellen Burstyn, four American families share their struggles in trying to cope with the demands of work and parenting. The scenarios include an Arkansas couple, white-collar professionals with two small sons; a Boston police officer, the single parent of a toddler; a couple living in rural New York who work varied swing shifts and have three children under the age of 2; and a divorced California couple sharing joint custody of their two children. Following the introduction, the program discusses important child care issues with legislators and business and community leaders. It includes interviews with Governor Bill Clinton of Arkansas, Senator Orrin Hatch, and Congressman George Miller, as well as pediatrician Dr. T. Berry Brazelton, Dr. Benjamin Spock, Bettye Caldwell, and Arnold Hiatt of Boston's StrideRite Corporation. A discussion guide accompanies the video.

McGruff's Self-Care Alert

Type: Video, 16mm film
Length: 17 minutes
Date: 1990
Cost: $295.00

Source: AIMS Media
6901 Woodley Avenue
Van Nuys, CA 91406
(818) 7854111

This video features McGruff the Crime Dog in four vignettes about latchkey children. Each vignette focuses on a basic rule for self-care: going straight home after school, checking for break-in signs, and the proper way to answer the phone when parents are not home. McGruff also offers suggestions on how latchkey kids can deal with loneliness and boredom.

Raising America's Children
Type: Video
Length: Ten 30-minute segments
Date: 1990
Cost: $749.00 for package of ten videotapes, $85.00 for individual tapes
Source: Delmar Publishers
2 Computer Drive West
Box 15015
Albany, NY 12212-5015
(800) 347-7707

This series, endorsed by the National Association for the Education of Young Children, examines child rearing during the early years and focuses on various stages of development in a wide variety of real-life settings. Titles in the series include *The Nurturing Community, A Secure Beginning, Relating to Others, Playing and Learning, Listening and Talking, Meeting Special Needs, Thinking and Creativity, Healthful Habits, Coping with Stress,* and *A Sense of Self.* An illustrated study guide is also available to accompany the series.

Safe and Sound: Choosing Quality Child Care
Type: Video
Length: 30 minutes
Date: 1991
Cost: $195.00
Source: Carle Medical Communications
110 West Main Street
Urbana, IL 61801-2700
(217) 384-4838

Narrated by actress Meredith Baxter Birney, this video offers helpful guidelines and examples of children and caregivers in ideal child care settings. The program is divided into seven segments dealing with various parental child care issues: "Finding Child Care," "Personal Interactions," "Education," "Health and Safety," "Communication and Consistency," "In-Home Care," and "Cost." National child care experts Helen Blank of the Children's Defense Fund and Ellen Galinsky of the Families and Work Institute provide insight into what parents should look for in a child care provider and the physical setting of a center. The accompanying parents' guide summarizes the points made in the video and offers a listing of national and state child care advocacy organizations.

Salaries, Working Conditions and the Teacher Shortage

Type: Video
Length: 17 minutes
Date: 1986
Cost: $39.00
Source: National Association for the Education of Young Children
1834 Connecticut Avenue, NW
Washington, DC 20009-5786
(800) 424-2460

This video is an advocacy tool that discusses the complex issues contributing to the crisis in recruitment and retention of qualified staff.

Selecting Daycare for Your Child

Type: Video
Length: 70 minutes
Date: 1990
Cost: $39.95
Source: Baker and Taylor
501 South Gladiolus
Momence, IL 60954
(800) 323-4243

This program looks at the status of child care in the United States and discusses the various reasons parents use child care situations. All of the common types of child care choices are explored in detail, including family child care, group homes, child care centers, nursery schools, preschools, nannies, and corporate facilities. A checklist for parents to use when visiting and evaluating different situations is included.

Spoonful of Lovin'

Type: Video
Length: Five 30-minute segments
Date: 1989
Cost: $775.00 for package of five videotapes, $180.00 for
individual tapes

Source: Delmar Publishers
                 2 Computer Drive West
                 Box 15015
                 Albany, NY 12212-5015
                 (800) 347-7707

This video training series for family child care providers covers topics such as child development basics, creative activities, child behavior guidance, room arrangements, safety, and parent-provider relationships. Series titles include *A Gourmet Guide to Family Home Day Care, Starting from Scratch—Birth to Three Years, Natural Ingredients—Development of the Preschool and School-Age Child, A Recipe for Happy Children,* and *A Good Measure of Safety.* Accompanying instructor's guide and student textbook are also available.

Techniques in Child Care: Planning and Operating a Quality Family Day Care Business
Type: Video
Length: 49 minutes
Date: 1990
Cost: $195.00
Source: Day Care Video Programs
               P.O. Box 396
               Boston, MA 02258
               (617) 646-9114

This how-to video explores family child care as a home-based business. The program discusses creating a safe, child-oriented environment, complying with state and federal regulations, participating in the USDA food program, and establishing good business practices in bookkeeping, marketing, and contract making. A highlight of the video is its interviews with family child care providers who openly discuss the pros and cons of establishing a family child care home business. A guidebook is included.

What Is Quality Child Care?
Type: Video
Length: Two tapes, one 53 minutes and one 57 minutes
Date: 1983
Cost: $39.00 for each tape
Source: National Association for the Education of Young Children
               1834 Connecticut Avenue, NW
               Washington, DC 20009-5786
               (800) 424-2460

These video presentations record papers presented at NAEYC's 1983 National Conference. Bettye M. Caldwell, Donaghey Distinguished Professor of Education at the University of Arkansas at Little Rock, and Asa G. Hilliard III, Fuller

E. Callaway Professor of Urban Education at Georgia State University, give their respective definitions of quality child care.

Worthy Work, Worthless Wages

Type: Video
Length: 15 minutes
Date: 1991
Cost: $12.95 plus shipping and handling
Source: Child Care Employee Project
6536 Telegraph Avenue, Suite A201
Oakland, CA 94618
(510) 653-9889

This is a video chronicle of the child care community activism that took place in Seattle, Washington, to improve the quality of services by confronting the staffing crisis. Included is footage of an April 1991 citywide child care center closure to protest low wages. The video documents the organizing strategies used in coordinating an annual child care parade and a day of closure that brought providers, parents, employers, and government together to explore solutions to this crisis. Also available is a discussion guide and packet of resource materials used in the organizing efforts.

Databases

BNA Plus

Cost: Varies by scope of service rendered
Source: Bureau of National Affairs
1231 Twenty-fifth Street, NW
Washington, DC 20037
(800) 452-7773

In addition to various other information services, BNA Plus performs confidential research, analysis, and monitoring of work- and family-related issues, compiles custom statistical reports on labor trends and activities, and provides a one-source document research and delivery service. No-obligation fee estimates are determined via a confidential conversation regarding the nature of requested research.

CareFinder

Cost: $500 for standard version, $700 for network version
Source: Work/Family Directions
930 Commonwealth Avenue South
Boston, MA 02215-1212
(800) 598-2256

This is a customized software system written for the functions of a child care resource and referral agency. It was designed to collect consistent national data, and to give resource and referral agencies customizable features for individual community needs. Capabilities include a child care provider search for parents that is fast, comprehensive, and uses a radial or linear geographic search based on map coordinates, customized data fields, reports on parent requests and provider supply, and mailing label capabilities.

Child Care Database

Cost: $395.00 annually plus connection time
Source: Executive Telecom System, Inc.
            College Park North
            9585 Valparaiso Court
            Indianapolis, IN 46209-6886
            (800) 421-8884

This database contains extensive information on approximately 1,700 child care programs in 40 states. Listings include such information as the name and address of the program, type of care offered, ages of children accepted, staff qualifications, curriculum, and year established.

Child Resource Information Bank (CRIB)

Cost: $5.00 CRIB guide
Source: International Child Resource Institute (ICRI)
            1810 Hopkins Street
            Berkeley, CA 94707
            (415) 644-1000

This database contains unpublished and published resources that have been collected from sources all over the world. This computer-based information source is open to public use.

Education Resources Information Center/Elementary and Early Childhood Education (ERIC/EECE)

Cost: Free
Source: ERIC/EECE
            University of Illinois at Urbana-Champaign
            805 West Pennsylvania Avenue
            Urbana, IL 61801
            (217) 333-1386

The ERIC system consists of 16 subject-specific clearinghouses and 4 support components that include research summaries, publications on topics of high interest, newsletters, and bibliographies. The EECE component covers social, psychological, physical, educational, and cultural development of children from the prenatal period through early adolescence, and theoretical and practical issues related to staff development, administration, curriculum, and parent or community factors affecting programs for children of this age group. Supported by the U.S. Department of Education, ERIC/EECE can be accessed on CD-ROM at many libraries and information centers.

Human Resource Information Network (HRIN)

Cost: Paid usage subscriptions begin at $980.00; include on-line time, telecom software package, training, user guide, toll-free customer support number, and monthly newsletter

Source: Executive Telecom Systems, Inc.
College Park North
9585 Valparaiso Court
Indianapolis, IN 46209-6886
(800) 421-8884

This network contains several databases that offer current information on work, family, quality of life, and other topics related to the effects of the changing work force. The Special Reports Library, an HRIN database, contains hundreds of reports, information sources, and compilations on a variety of human resource issues. Reports of particular applicability to child care research are *Corporations and Families, Changing Practices and Perspectives, Child Care in the 100th Congress, Legislation and Policy Issues,* and *101 Key Statistics on Work and Family for the 1990's.*

LEGISNET

Cost: Free
Source: National Conference of State Legislators
1050 Seventeenth Street, Suite 2100
Denver, CO 80265
(303) 623-7800

Abstracts of thousands of legislative research reports, public policy documents, state surveys, and statistical information are available to state legislators and their staffs via this system.

Quality of Worklife Database (QWLD)

Cost: $81 per connect hour (basic plan)
Source: Management Directions
P.O. Box 26987
Austin, TX 78755
(512) 331-0224

This database provides bibliographic listings and literature abstracts covering work and family life topics such as alternatives to traditional work arrangements, dual-career families, health and wellness, child care, and statistics and trends. Information is compiled from more than 300 sources, including journals, newspapers, books, reports, conference proceedings, corporate publications, and magazines.

State-by-State
Child Care Profiles

THIS CHAPTER PRESENTS BASIC INFORMATION about the regulatory status of each of the individual states. Following are descriptions of the categories included for each state:

State regulatory agency: An address is given for the state government agency charged with establishing and implementing policies and regulations governing various types of child care.

Statewide resource and referral network: Community resource and referral agencies are sources of comprehensive information about child care resources within a given geographic area; the state network generally serves as an "umbrella" office and as a clearinghouse of information for community-based resource and referral agencies. This listing includes the statewide network office whenever possible. In states where there is no network office, community-based offices are listed (these states are designated with asterisks).

Features of child care center regulation:

Child:staff ratios: The National Association for the Education of Young Children (NAEYC) has established the following guidelines for optimal child:staff ratios. For 1-year-olds, a ratio of one caregiver to every three or four children is preferred. For 3-year-olds, a ratio of one caregiver to every seven to ten children is preferred. For 5-year-olds, a ratio of one caregiver to every eight to ten children is preferred.

Number of inspections per year: This involves inspections by officials of the state regulatory agency to ensure that individual centers and programs are in compliance with established regulations.

Training required: Research has shown a direct correlation between the amount of child care-related training staff members receive and the quality of care given. Specific training requirements for child care workers vary widely among states. Most, however, require some form of preservice training (including college-level courses), health, and/or first-aid training.

Criminal record check: As part of the licensing/registry screening process, many states cross-check child care provider applicants against the state's convicted criminal records.

Child abuse record check: As part of the licensing/registry screening process, many states cross-check child care provider applicants for confirmed charges of child abuse within the state.

Features of family child care regulation:

Definition: This is a description of how the state defines family child care for regulatory purposes. Many experts agree that one family child care provider should care for no more than six preschool children, with no more than two of those children under the age of 2. Most states require two providers for group home situations.

Type of regulation: This item tells whether a state requires mandatory or voluntary registration or licensing processes for family child care providers.

Number of inspections per year: This involves inspections by officials of the state regulatory agency to ensure that individual centers and programs are in compliance with established regulations.

Training required: Research has shown a direct correlation between the amount of child care-related training staff members receive and the quality of care given.

Criminal record check: As part of the licensing/registry screening process, many states cross-check child care provider applicants against the state's convicted criminal records.

Child abuse record check: As part of the licensing/registry screening process, many states cross-check child care provider applicants for confirmed charges of child abuse within the state.

Alabama

State Regulatory Agency

Department of Human Resources
64 North Union Street
Montgomery, AL 36130
(205) 261-5360

Statewide Resource and Referral Network

Alabama Association for Child Care Resource and Referral Agencies
309 North 23rd Street
Birmingham, AL 35203
(205) 252-1991

Features of Child Care Center Regulation

Child:staff ratios:	1-year-olds, 6:1
	3-year-olds, 12:1
	5-year-olds, 20:1
Number of inspections per year:	1
Training required:	Preservice
Criminal record check?	Yes
Child abuse record check?	No

Features of Family Child Care Regulation

Definition:	1–6 children = family child care; 7–12 = group home
Type of regulation:	License
Number of inspections per year:	1
Training required:	4 hours of training in child development every 2 years
Criminal record check?	Yes
Child abuse record check?	No

Alaska

State Regulatory Agency

Department of Health and Human Services
Division of Family and Youth Services
230 South Franklin Street
Juneau, AK 99801
(907) 465-3013

Statewide Resource and Referral Network

Alaska Child Care Resource and Referral Alliance
P.O. Box 10339
Anchorage, AK 99510
(907) 279-5024

Features of Child Care Center Regulation

Child:staff ratios:	1-year-olds, 6:1
	3-year-olds, 10:1
	5-year-olds, 15:1
Number of inspections per year:	1 per 2 years
Training required:	None
Criminal record check?	No
Child abuse record check?	No

Features of Family Child Care Regulation

Definition:	1–10 children under age 12 = family child care, including provider's children; maximum of 2 under 30 months
Type of regulation:	License
Number of inspections per year:	1 per 2 years
Training required:	None
Criminal record check?	No
Child abuse record check?	No

Arizona

State Regulatory Agency

Department of Health Services
Office of Children Day Care Facilities
801 East Jefferson
Phoenix, AZ 85034
(602) 255-1272

Statewide Resource and Referral Network*

Association for Supportive Child Care
2510 South Rural Road, Suite J
Tempe, AZ 85282
(602) 829-0500

Family Service Agency
1530 East Flower
Phoenix, AZ 85014
(602) 264-9891

Tucson Association for Child Care, Inc.
1030 North Alvernon Way
Tucson, AZ 85711
(602) 881-8940

Features of Child Care Center Regulation

Child:staff ratios:

1-year-olds, 6:1
3-year-olds, 13:1
5-year-olds, 20:1

Number of inspections per year: 2
Training required: Preservice and health training
Criminal record check?   Yes
Child abuse record check?   No

Features of Family Child Care Regulation

Definition:

No guidelines for unsubsidized family child care; 5–10 = group home, including provider's children under 14 years

Type of regulation: Registration
Number of inspections per year: 2
Training required: None
Criminal record check?   Yes
Child abuse record check?   Yes

Arkansas

State Regulatory Agency

Division of Children and Family Services
Day Care Licensing
P.O. Box 1437
Little Rock, AR 72203
(501) 682-8590

Statewide Resource and Referral Network

Arkansas Child Care Resource and Referral Center
5 Statehouse Plaza
Little Rock, AR 72201
(501) 375-3690

Features of Child Care Center Regulation

Child:staff ratios:	1-year-olds, 6:1
	3-year-olds, 12:1
	5-year-olds, 18:1
Number of inspections per year:	3–4
Training required:	Preservice
Criminal record check?	No
Child abuse record check?	No

Features of Family Child Care Regulation

Definition:	1–6 = family child care, including provider's preschoolers, maximum of 3 under 2 years; 7–12 = group home, maximum of 4 under 2 years
Type of regulation:	Voluntary license for family child care; license for group home
Number of inspections per year:	3–4
Training required:	6 hours of ongoing training each year
Criminal record check?	No
Child abuse record check?	No

California

State Regulatory Agency

Department of Social Services
Day Care Unit
744 P Street
Mail Station 19-50
Sacramento, CA 95814
(916) 324-4031

Statewide Resource and Referral Network

California Child Care Resource and Referral Network
809 Lincoln Way
San Francisco, CA 94122
(415) 661-1714

Features of Child Care Center Regulation

Child:staff ratios:	1-year-olds, 4:1
	3-year-olds, 12:1
	5-year-olds, 12:1
Number of inspections per year:	1
Training required:	Preservice
Criminal record check?	Yes
Child abuse record check?	Yes

Features of Family Child Care Regulation

Definition:	2–6 = family child care, maximum of 3 under 2 years, or 4 if all are infants; 7–12 = group home, maximum of 4 under 2 years
Type of regulation:	License
Number of inspections per year:	10% sample
Training required:	None
Criminal record check?	Yes
Child abuse record check?	Yes

Colorado

State Regulatory Agency

Department of Social Services
Office of Child Care Services
1575 Sherman Street
Denver, CO 80203-1714
(303) 866-5958

Statewide Resource and Referral Network

Colorado Resource and Referral Network
7853 E. Arapahoe Road, Suite 3300
Englewood, CO 80112
(303) 290-9088

Features of Child Care Center Regulation

Child:staff ratios:	1-year-olds, 5:1
	3-year-olds, 10:1
	5-year-olds, 15:1
Number of inspections per year:	1 per 2 years
Training required:	Preservice and first-aid training
Criminal record check?	Yes
Child abuse record check?	Yes

Features of Family Child Care Regulation

Definition:	4 under 30 months = infant/toddler home; 2–6 = family child care, maximum of 2 under 2 years; 7–12 = group home, maximum of 6 under 2 years
Type of regulation:	License
Number of inspections per year:	33% sample
Training required:	6 hours of training in child care-related topics
Criminal record check?	Yes
Child abuse record check?	Yes

Connecticut

State Regulatory Agency

State Department of Health Services
150 Washington Street
Hartford, CT 06106
(203) 566-2575

Statewide Resource and Referral Network*

Region 1

Southwest Child Care Info Line
83 East Avenue, Room 107
Norwalk, CT 06851
(203) 333-7555

Region 2

South Central Child Care Info Line
One State Street
New Haven, CT 06511
(203) 624-4143

Region 3

Southeast Child Care Info Line
74 West Main Street
Norwich, CT 06360
(203) 346-6691

Region 4

North Central Child Care Info Line
900 Asylum Avenue
Hartford, CT 06105
(203) 482-9471

Region 5

Northwest Child Care Info Line
232 North Elm Street
Waterbury, CT 06702
(203) 482-9471

Region 6

Northeast Child Care Info Line
948 Main Street
Willimantic, CT 06226
(203) 456-8886

Features of Child Care Center Regulation

Child:staff ratios:	1-year-olds, 4:1
	3-year-olds, 10:1
	5-year-olds, 10:1
Number of inspections per year:	1 per 2 years
Training required:	Preservice and first-aid training
Criminal record check?	Yes
Child abuse record check?	No

Features of Family Child Care Regulation

Definition:	1–6 = family child care, maximum of 2 under 2 years, including provider's preschoolers; 7–12 = group home
Type of regulation:	Registration for family child care; license for group home
Number of inspections per year:	1 per 2 years
Training required:	None
Criminal record check?	Yes
Child abuse record check?	Yes

Delaware

State Regulatory Agency

Licensing Bureau, Youth and Family Division
1825 Faulkland Road
Wilmington, DE 19805-1195
(302) 633-2700

Statewide Resource and Referral Network

Child Care Connection
3411 Silverside Road, Barnard 100
Wilmington, DE 19810
(302) 479-1660

Features of Child Care Center Regulation

Child:staff ratios:	1-year-olds, 7:1
	3-year-olds, 12:1
	5-year-olds, 25:1
Number of inspections per year:	1
Training required:	Preservice and first-aid training
Criminal record check?	No
Child abuse record check?	Yes

Features of Family Child Care Regulation

Definition:	1–6 = family child care, maximum of 4 under 2 years, including provider's preschoolers; 7–11 = group home, maximum of 4 under 2 years
Type of regulation:	License
Number of inspections per year:	1
Training required:	6 hours of orientation
Criminal record check?	No
Child abuse record check?	Yes

Florida

State Regulatory Agency

Department of Health and Rehabilitation Services
Office of Children, Youth and Families
1317 Winewood Boulevard
Building 6, Room 1014
Tallahassee, FL 32399
(904) 488-4900

Statewide Resource and Referral Agency

Florida Child Care Resource and Referral Network
1282 Paul Russell Road
Tallahassee, FL 32301
(904) 656-2272

Features of Child Care Center Regulation

Child:staff ratios:	1-year-olds, 8:1
	3-year-olds, 15:1
	5-year-olds, 25:1
Number of inspections per year:	4
Training required:	Preservice, health, and first-aid training
Criminal record check?	Yes
Child abuse record check?	Yes

Features of Family Child Care Regulation

Definition:	2–5 = family child care, including provider's preschoolers
Type of regulation:	License or registration by authorized county
Number of inspections per year:	2
Training required:	3 hours of training in child care
Criminal record check?	Yes
Child abuse record check?	Yes

Georgia

State Regulatory Agency

Department of Human Resources
Child Care Licensing Office
878 Peachtree Street, NE, Room 607
Atlanta, GA 30309
(404) 894-5688

Statewide Resource and Referral Network*

Care Connection
850 College Station Road, No. 332
Athens, GA 30610
(404) 353-1313

Care Solutions, Inc.
5 Concourse Parkway, Suite 810
Atlanta, GA 30328
(404) 393-7366

Child Care Solutions of North Georgia
Gainesville College
Gainesville, GA 30503
(404) 535-6383

Save the Children/Child Care Solutions
1340 Spring Street, NW, Suite 200
Atlanta, GA 30309
(404) 885-1585

Features of Child Care Center Regulation

Child:staff ratios:	1-year-olds, 7:1
	3-year-olds, 15:1
	5-year-olds, 20:1
Number of inspections per year:	4
Training required:	Preservice
Criminal record check?	Yes
Child abuse record check?	No

Features of Family Child Care Regulation

Definition:	3–6 = family child care, including provider's children; 7–18 = group home, maximum of 10 under 30 months
Type of regulation:	Registration for family child care; license for group home
Number of inspections per year:	3% sample
Training required:	First-aid training
Criminal record check?	Yes
Child abuse record check?	No

Hawaii

State Regulatory Agency

Department of Human Resources
Licensing Unit
420 Weiaka Milo Road, Suite 101
Honolulu, HI 96817-4941
(808) 832-5025

Statewide Resource and Referral Network

Parents Attentive to Children (PATCH)
810 North Vineyard Boulevard
Honolulu, HI 96717
(808) 842-3874

Features of Child Care Center Regulation

Child:staff ratios:	1-year-olds, minimum age of 2 years for center care; 3-year-olds, 12:1; 5-year-olds, 20:1
Number of inspections per year:	1–3
Training required:	Preservice and health training
Criminal record check?	Yes
Child abuse record check?	No

Features of Family Child Care Regulation

Definition:	2–6 = family child care, maximum of 2 under 2 years, including provider's children under 6 years; 7–12 = group home, maximum of 4 under 18 months
Type of regulation:	Registration for family child care; license for group home
Number of inspections per year:	1
Training required:	Ongoing training each year in 2 of 12 state-specified areas
Criminal record check?	Yes
Child abuse record check?	No

Idaho

State Regulatory Agency

Department of Health and Welfare
Family and Children's Division
4355 Emerald Street
Boise, ID 83706
(208) 334-6800

Statewide Resource and Referral Network*

Child Care Choices, Inc.
1000 West Garden
Coeur d'Alene, ID 83814
(208) 765-6296

Child Care Connections
P.O. Box 6756
Boise, ID 83707
(208) 343-KIDS

Human Services Center, Inc.
3100 Rollandet
Idaho Falls, ID 83403
(208) 525-7281

Southeast Idaho Community Action Agency
P.O. Box 940
Pocatello, ID 83204
(208) 232-1114

Features of Child Care Center Regulation

Child:staff ratios:	1-year-olds, 12:1
	3-year-olds, 12:1
	5-year-olds, 12:1
Number of inspections per year:	1
Training required:	None
Criminal record check?	Yes
Child abuse record check?	No

Features of Family Child Care Regulation

Definition: 2–6 = family child care, not
including provider's children; 7–12
= group home

Type of regulation: Voluntary license
Number of inspections per year: 1
Training required: None
Criminal record check?   No
Child abuse record check?   No

Illinois

State Regulatory Agency

Department of Children and Family Services
406 East Monroe Avenue
Springfield, IL 62701-1498
(217) 785-2598

Statewide Resource and Referral Network

Illinois Child Care Resource and Referral System
100 West Randolph, Suite 16-206
Chicago, IL 60601
(312) 814-5524

Features of Child Care Center Regulation

Child:staff ratios: 1-year-olds, 4:1
3-year-olds, 12:1
5-year-olds, 12:1
Number of inspections per year: 1
Training required: Preservice
Criminal record check?   Yes
Child abuse record check?   Yes

Features of Family Child Care Regulation

Definition:	4–8 = family child care, maximum of 3 under 2 years, including provider's children under 14 years; 4–12 = group home, maximum of 6 under 30 months
Type of regulation:	License
Number of inspections per year:	1
Training required:	None
Criminal record check?	Yes
Child abuse record check?	Yes

Indiana

State Regulatory Agency

Department of Public Welfare
Child Welfare/Social Services Division
141 South Meridian Street, 6th Floor
Indianapolis, IN 46225
(317) 232-4440

Statewide Resource and Referral Network

Indiana Association for Child Care Resource and Referral
4460 Guion Road
Indianapolis, IN 46254
(317) 299-2750

Features of Child Care Center Regulation

Child:staff ratios:	1-year-olds, 5:1
	3-year-olds, 10:1
	5-year-olds, 15:1
Number of inspections per year:	3
Training required:	Preservice and first-aid training
Criminal record check?	No
Child abuse record check?	No

Features of Family Child Care Regulation

Definition: 5–10 = family child care,
                                       maximum of 6 under 2 years,
                                       including provider's children
                                       under 11 years
Type of regulation: License
Number of inspections per year: 1
Training required: None
Criminal record check?   No
Child abuse record check?   No

Iowa

State Regulatory Agency

Department of Human Services
Hoover Building, 5th Floor
Des Moines, IA 50319
(515) 281-6074

Statewide Resource and Referral Network

Iowa Commission on Children, Youth and Families
Department of Human Rights, Lucas Building
Des Moines, IA 50319
(515) 281-3974

Features of Child Care Center Regulation

Child:staff ratios: 1-year-olds, 4:1
                                       3-year-olds, 8:1
                                       5-year-olds, 15:1
Number of inspections per year: 1
Training required: Preservice
Criminal record check?   Yes
Child abuse record check?   Yes

Features of Family Child Care Regulation

Definition:	1–6 = family child care, maximum of 4 under 2 years, including provider's preschoolers; 7–11 = group home, maximum of 4 under 2 years
Type of regulation:	Voluntary registration for family child care; mandatory registration for group home
Number of inspections per year:	20% sample
Training required:	None
Criminal record check?	Yes
Child abuse record check?	Yes

Kansas

State Regulatory Agency

Department of Health and Environment
Landon State Office Building
Child Care Licensing Section
900 Southwest Jackson Street
Topeka, KS 66612-1290
(913) 296-1275

Statewide Resource and Referral Network*

Child Care Association
1069 Parkland Office Park
Wichita, KS 67218
(316) 682-1853

Everywoman's Resource Center
1002 Southwest Garfield, Suite 109
Topeka, KS 66604
(913) 357-5171

Heart of America Family Service
8047 Parallel Parkway
Kansas City, KS 66112
(816) 753-5280

Features of Child Care Center Regulation

Child:staff ratios:	1-year-olds, 5:1
	3-year-olds, 10:1/12:1
	5-year-olds, 14:1
Number of inspections per year:	Unknown
Training required:	Preservice and health training
Criminal record check?	Yes
Child abuse record check?	Yes

Features of Family Child Care Regulation

Definition:	1–10 = family child care, maximum of 3 under 18 months, including provider's children under 16 years; 7–12 = group home, maximum of 3 infants and toddlers
Type of regulation:	Registration or voluntary license for family child care; license for group home
Number of inspections per year:	Unknown
Training required:	None
Criminal record check?	Yes
Child abuse record check?	Yes

Kentucky

State Regulatory Agency

Cabinet for Human Resources
Division of Licensing and Regulation
275 East Main Street
Frankfort, KY 40621
(502) 564-2800

Statewide Resource and Referral Network*

Child Care Council of Kentucky
800 Sparta Court, No. 100
Lexington, KY 40504
(606) 254-9176

Community Coordinated Child Care
1215 South Third Street
Louisville, KY 40203
(502) 636-1358

Kentucky Coalition for School Age Child Care
200 High Street
Bowling Green, KY 42101
(502) 842-4281

Features of Child Care Center Regulation

Child:staff ratios:	1-year-olds, 6:1
	3-year-olds, 12:1
	5-year-olds, 15:1
Number of inspections per year:	1
Training required:	Health training
Criminal record check?	Yes
Child abuse record check?	No

Features of Family Child Care Regulation

Definition:	4–12 family child care (Type II facility), maximum of 6 under age 2, including provider's children
Type of regulation:	License
Number of inspections per year:	1
Training required:	None
Criminal record check?	Yes
Child abuse record check?	No

Louisiana

State Regulatory Agency

Department of Health and Hospitals
Division of Licensing and Certification
P.O. Box 3767
Baton Rouge, LA 70821
(504) 342-6446

Statewide Resource and Referral Network*

Child Care Information, Inc.
P.O. Box 45212, D-223
Baton Rouge, LA 70895
(504) 293-8523

Child Care Resources
P.O. Box 51837
New Orleans, LA 70151
(504) 586-8509

Child Care Services of NW Louisiana
209 Milam, Suite C
Shreveport, LA 71101-7728
(318) 227-1812

Features of Child Care Center Regulation

Child:staff ratios:	1-year-olds, 8:1
	3-year-olds, 14:1
	5-year-olds, 20:1
Number of inspections per year:	1
Training required:	None
Criminal record check?	No
Child abuse record check?	No

Features of Family Child Care Regulation

Definition:	No state definitions currently exist
Type of regulation:	No state regulations currently exist
Number of inspections per year:	0
Training required:	None
Criminal record check?	Yes
Child abuse record check?	No

Maine

State Regulatory Agency

Department of Human Services
Bureau of Child and Family Services
221 State Street
Augusta, ME 04333
(207) 289-5060

Statewide Resource and Referral Network

Maine Association of Child Care Resource and Referral Agencies
P.O. Box 280-WHCA
Millbridge, ME 04658
(207) 546-7544

Features of Child Care Center Regulation

Child:staff ratios:	1-year-olds, 4:1
	3-year-olds, 10:1
	5-year-olds, 10:1
Number of inspections per year:	1
Training required:	Preservice
Criminal record check?	Yes
Child abuse record check?	No

Features of Family Child Care Regulation

Definition:	3–12 = family child care, maximum of 4 under age 2, including provider's preschoolers
Type of regulation:	License
Number of inspections per year:	1
Training required:	None
Criminal record check?	No
Child abuse record check?	Yes

Maryland

State Regulatory Agency

Office of Licensing and Certification
Division of Child Care Centers
4201 Patterson Avenue
Baltimore, MD 21215
(301) 764-2750

Statewide Resource and Referral Network

Maryland Child Care Resource Network
608 Water Street
Baltimore, MD 21202
(303) 752-7588

Features of Child Care Center Regulation

Child:staff ratios:	1-year-olds, 3:1 3-year-olds, 10:1 5-year-olds, 13:1
Number of inspections per year:	1
Training required:	Preservice and health training
Criminal record check?	No
Child abuse record check?	No

Features of Family Child Care Regulation

Definition:	1–6 = family child care, maximum of 2 under 2 years, including provider's infants
Type of regulation:	Registration
Number of inspections per year:	1
Training required:	None
Criminal record check?	No
Child abuse record check?	No

Massachusetts

State Regulatory Agency

Office for Children
10 West Street
Boston, MA 02111
(617) 727-8956

Statewide Resource and Referral Network

Massachusetts Office for Children
10 West Street, 5th Floor
Boston, MA 02111
(617) 727-8900

Features of Child Care Center Regulation

Child:staff ratios:	1-year-olds, 3:1/7:2 3-year-olds, 10:1/12:1 5-year-olds, 15:1
Number of inspections per year:	Unknown
Training required:	Preservice, health, and first-aid training
Criminal record check?	Yes
Child abuse record check?	Yes

Features of Family Child Care Regulation

Definition:	1–6 = family day care, maximum of 2 under age 2, including provider's children under 10 years
Type of regulation:	License
Number of inspections per year:	Unknown
Training required:	None
Criminal record check?	Yes
Child abuse record check?	Yes

Michigan

State Regulatory Agency

Department of Social Services
Division of Child Day Care Licensing
235 South Grand Street
P.O. Box 30037
Lansing, MI 48909
(517) 373-8300

Statewide Resource and Referral Network

Michigan Community Coordinated Child Care (4C) Association
2875 Northwind Drive, No. 200
East Lansing, MI 48823
(517) 351-4171

Features of Child Care Center Regulation

Child:staff ratios:	1-year-olds, 4:1
	3-year-olds, 10:1
	5-year-olds, 12:1
Number of inspections per year:	1
Training required:	Preservice and health
Criminal record check?	Yes
Child abuse record check?	Yes

Features of Family Child Care Regulation

Definition:	1–6 = family child care, maximum of 4 under 30 months, including provider's preschoolers; 7–12 = group home, maximum of 8 under 30 months
Type of regulation:	Registration for family child care; license for group homes
Number of inspections per year:	0
Training required:	First-aid and CPR within first 3 years
Criminal record check?	Yes
Child abuse record check?	Yes

Minnesota

State Regulatory Agency

Department of Human Services
Division of Licensing
444 LaFayette Road
Saint Paul, MN 55155
(612) 296-3971

Statewide Resource and Referral Network

Minnesota Child Care Resource and Referral Network
2116 Campus Drive, SE
Rochester, MN 55904
(507) 287-2497

Features of Child Care Center Regulation

Child:staff ratios:	1-year-olds, 4:1
	3-year-olds, 10:1
	5-year-olds, 10:1
Number of inspections per year:	Unknown
Training required:	Preservice, health, and first-aid training
Criminal record check?	Yes
Child abuse record check?	Yes

Features of Family Child Care Regulation

Definition:	2–10 = family child care, maximum of 3 under 30 months, including provider's children; 2–14 = group home, maximum of 4 under 30 months
Type of regulation:	License
Number of inspections per year:	Unknown
Training required:	6 hours of child care training and first-aid training in first year
Criminal record check?	Yes
Child abuse record check?	Yes

Mississippi

State Regulatory Agency

Department of Health
Division of Child Care and Special Licensure
P.O. Box 1700
Jackson, MS 39215-1700
(601) 960-7504

Features of Child Care Center Regulation

Child:staff ratios:	1-year-olds, 9:1
	3-year-olds, 14:1
	5-year-olds, 20:1
Number of inspections per year:	2
Training required:	None
Criminal record check?	Yes
Child abuse record check?	No

Features of Family Child Care Regulation

Definition:	No family child care designation; 6–15 = group home, maximum of 9 under 2 years, not including provider's children
Type of regulation:	License
Number of inspections per year:	2
Training required:	None
Criminal record check?	Yes
Child abuse record check?	No

Missouri

State Regulatory Agency

Department of Social Services
Office of Child Care Licensing
P.O. Box 88
Jefferson City, MO 65103
(314) 751-2450

Statewide Resource and Referral Network*

Child Day Care Association
915 Olive, Suite 913
St. Louis, MO 63101
(314) 241-3161

Heart of America Family Services
3217 Broadway, Suite 500
Kansas City, MO 64111
(816) 753-5280

Features of Child Care Center Regulation

Child:staff ratios:	1-year-olds, 4:1
	3-year-olds, 10:1
	5-year-olds, 16:1
Number of inspections per year:	2
Training required:	Preservice
Criminal record check?	No
Child abuse record check?	Yes

Features of Family Child Care Regulation

Definition:	5–10 = family child care
Type of regulation:	License
Number of inspections per year:	2
Training required:	None
Criminal record check?	No
Child abuse record check?	Yes

Montana

State Regulatory Agency

Department of Family Services
P.O. Box 8005
Helena, MT 59604
(406) 444-5900

Statewide Resource and Referral Network*

Child Care Connections
321 East Main, Suite 423
Bozeman, MT 59715
(406) 587-7786

Human Resources Development Council
P.O. Box 2016
Billings, MT 59103
(406) 248-1477

Features of Child Care Center Regulation

Child:staff ratios:	1-year-olds, 4:1
	3-year-olds, 8:1
	5-year-olds, 25:1
Number of inspections per year:	1
Training required:	Preservice and health training
Criminal record check?	No
Child abuse record check?	No

Features of Family Child Care Regulation

Definition:	1–6 = family child care, maximum of 3 under 2 years, including provider's children under 6 years; 7–12 = group home, maximum of 6 under 2 years
Type of regulation:	License
Number of inspections per year:	15% sample
Training required:	None
Criminal record check?	No
Child abuse record check?	No

Nebraska

State Regulatory Agency

Department of Social Services
P.O. Box 95026
Lincoln, NE 68509
(402) 471-3121

Statewide Resource and Referral Network

Midwest Child Care Association
5015 Dodge, Suite 2
Omaha, NE 68132
(402) 551-2379

Features of Child Care Center Regulation

Child:staff ratios:	1-year-olds, 4:1
	3-year-olds, 10:1
	5-year-olds, 15:1
Number of inspections per year:	2
Training required:	Preservice and first-aid training
Criminal record check?	No
Child abuse record check?	Yes

Features of Family Child Care Regulation

Definition:	4–8 = family child care, maximum of 2 under 18 months, including provider's preschoolers; 4–12 = group home, maximum of 4 under 18 months
Type of regulation:	Registration for family child care; license for group home
Number of inspections per year:	5% per month
Training required:	None
Criminal record check?	No
Child abuse record check?	Yes

Nevada

State Regulatory Agency

Bureau of Services for Child Care
505 East King Street, Room 101
Carson City, NV 89710
(702) 885-5911

Statewide Resource and Referral Network

Child Care Resource Council
1090 South Rock Boulevard
Reno, NV 89502
(702) 785-4200

Features of Child Care Center Regulation

Child:staff ratios:	1-year-olds, 6:1
	3-year-olds, 13:1
	5-year-olds, 13:1
Number of inspections per year:	4
Training required:	Preservice, health, and first-aid training
Criminal record check?	Yes
Child abuse record check?	No

Features of Family Child Care Regulation

Definition:	5–6 = family child care, maximum of 4 under 2 years, not including provider's children; 7–12 = group home, maximum of 8 under 2 years
Type of regulation:	License
Number of inspections per year:	4
Training required:	3 hours of approved training each year
Criminal record check?	Yes
Child abuse record check?	No

New Hampshire

State Regulatory Agency

Division of Public Health Services
Bureau of Child Care Licensing
Health and Human Services Building
6 Hazen Drive
Concord, NH 03301
(603) 271-4624

Statewide Resource and Referral Network

New Hampshire Association of Child Care Resource and Referral Agencies
99 Hanover Street
P.O. Box 448
Manchester, NH 03105
(603) 668-1920

Features of Child Care Center Regulation

Child:staff ratios:	1-year-olds, 5:1
	3-year-olds, 8:1
	5-year-olds, 15:1
Number of inspections per year:	3 per 2 years
Training required:	Preservice and health training
Criminal record check?	Yes
Child abuse record check?	No

Features of Family Child Care Regulation

Definition:	4–6 = family child care, maximum of 2 under 2 years, including provider's children under 6 years; 7–12 = group home, maximum of 4 under 2 years
Type of regulation:	License
Number of inspections per year:	3 per 2 years
Training required:	18–21-year-olds must have an unspecified amount of training
Criminal record check?	Yes
Child abuse record check?	No

New Jersey

State Regulatory Agency

Bureau of Licensing
Division of Youth and Family Services
CN717
Trenton, NJ 08625-0717
(609) 291-1021 (north); (609)292-9220 (south)

Statewide Resource and Referral Network

Statewide Clearinghouse
Division of Youth and Family Services
Capitol Center
50 East State Street, CN 717
Trenton, NJ 08625
(609) 292-8408

Features of Child Care Center Regulation

Child:staff ratios:	1-year-olds, 4:1
	3-year-olds, 10:1
	5-year-olds, 15:1
Number of inspections per year:	1 per 3 years
Training required:	Preservice and health training
Criminal record check?	No
Child abuse record check?	No

Features of Family Child Care Regulation

Definition:	1–6 = family child care, maximum of 4 under 2 years, not including provider's children
Type of regulation:	Voluntary registration
Number of inspections per year:	1 per 3 years
Training required:	Training sessions twice per year
Criminal record check?	No
Child abuse record check?	No

New Mexico

State Regulatory Agency

Public Health Division
Licensing, Health-Related Facilities
1190 Saint Francis, Room North 1300
Santa Fe, NM 87503
(505) 827-2448

Statewide Resource and Referral Network*

Child Care Resource and Referral Project
Santa Fe Community College
P.O. Box 4187
Santa Fe, NM 87502-4187
(505) 438-1344

Las Cruces Child Care Resource and Referral
Box 30001, Department 3R
Las Cruces, NM 88003
(505) 646-1165

Roswell Child Care Resource and Referral
P.O. Box 3038
Roswell, NM 88202
(505) 622-9000

Features of Child Care Center Regulation

Child:staff ratios:	1-year-olds, 6:1
	3-year-olds, 12:1
	5-year-olds, 15:1
Number of inspections per year:	2
Training required:	Preservice and first-aid training
Criminal record check?	Yes
Child abuse record check?	No

Features of Family Child Care Regulation

Definition:	5–6 = family child care, maximum of 2 under 2 years, including provider's children; 7–12 = group home, maximum of 4 under age 2
Type of regulation:	License
Number of inspections per year:	2
Training required:	6 hours of training per year
Criminal record check?	Yes
Child abuse record check?	No

New York

State Regulatory Agency

Department of Social Services
40 North Pearl Street
Albany, NY 12243
(800) 342-3715

Statewide Resource and Referral Network

New York State Child Care Coordinating Council
237 Bradford Street
Albany, NY 12206
(518) 463-8663

Features of Child Care Center Regulation

Child:staff ratios:	1-year-olds, 4:1
	3-year-olds, 6:1/7:1
	5-year-olds, 8:1/9:1
Number of inspections per year:	1
Training required:	Preservice and health training
Criminal record check?	No
Child abuse record check?	Yes

Features of Family Child Care Regulation

Definition:	3–6 = family child care, maximum of 2 under 2 years, not including provider's children; 7–12 = group home, maximum of 4 under 2 years
Type of regulation:	License
Number of inspections per year:	1
Training required:	None
Criminal record check?	No
Child abuse record check?	Yes

North Carolina

State Regulatory Agency

Office of Child Day Care Licensing
Child Day Care Section
701 Balbour Drive
Raleigh, NC 27603-2008
(919) 733-4801

Statewide Resource and Referral Network

North Carolina Child Care Resource and Referral Network
700 Kenilworth Avenue
Charlotte, NC 28204
(704) 376-6697

Features of Child Care Center Regulation

Child:staff ratios:	1-year-olds, 7:1
	3-year-olds, 15:1
	5-year-olds, 25:1
Number of inspections per year:	3
Training required:	Preservice and first-aid training
Criminal record check?	No
Child abuse record check?	No

Features of Family Child Care Regulation

Definition:	3–8 = family child care, maximum of 3 under 2 years, including provider's children under 6 years; 6–12 = group home, maximum of 12 under 3 years
Type of regulation:	Registration for family child care; license for group home
Number of inspections per year:	Unknown
Training required:	None
Criminal record check?	No
Child abuse record check?	No

North Dakota

State Regulatory Agency

Department of Human Services
Children and Family Services
600 East Boulevard Avenue
Bismarck, ND 58505-0268
(701) 224-3580

Statewide Resource and Referral Network

Early Childhood Training Center
North Dakota State University
P.O. Box 5057
State University Station
Fargo, ND 58105
(701) 237-8040

Features of Child Care Center Regulation

Child:staff ratios:	1-year-olds, 4:1
	3-year-olds, 7:1
	5-year-olds, 12:1
Number of inspections per year:	2
Training required:	Preservice and health training
Criminal record check?	No
Child abuse record check?	Yes

Features of Family Child Care Regulation

Definition:	4–7 = family child care, maximum of 4 under 2 years, including provider's children under 12 years; 8–18 = group home, maximum of 8 under 2 years
Type of regulation:	License
Number of inspections per year:	2
Training required:	5 hours of training each year
Criminal record check?	No
Child abuse record check?	Yes

Ohio

State Regulatory Agency

Office of Child Care Services
30 East Broad Street, 30th Floor
Columbus, OH 43215
(614) 466-3822

Statewide Resource and Referral Network

Ohio Child Care Resource and Referral Association
92 Jefferson Avenue
Columbus, OH 43215
(614) 224-0222

Features of Child Care Center Regulation

Child:staff ratios:	1-year-olds, 6:1
	3-year-olds, 12:1
	5-year-olds, 14:1
Number of inspections per year:	2
Training required:	Preservice and first-aid training
Criminal record check?	No
Child abuse record check?	No

Features of Family Child Care Regulation

Definition:	1–6 = family child care, maximum of 3 under 2 years, including provider's children under 6 years; 7–12 = group home, maximum of 8 under 18 months
Type of regulation:	Voluntary license for family day care; license for group home
Number of inspections per year:	2
Training required:	None
Criminal record check?	No
Child abuse record check?	No

Oklahoma

State Regulatory Agency

Department of Human Services
Child Care Licensing Unit
P.O. Box 25352
Oklahoma City, OK 73125
(405) 521-3561

Statewide Resource and Referral Network

Child Care Connection
3014 Paseo
Oklahoma City, OK 73101
(405) 525-3111

Child Care Resource Center
1430 South Boulder
Tulsa, OK 74119
(918) 587-CARE

Features of Child Care Center Regulation

Child:staff ratios:	1-year-olds, 6:1
	3-year-olds, 12:1
	5-year-olds, 15:1
Number of inspections per year:	4
Training required:	Preservice
Criminal record check?	No
Child abuse record check?	No

Features of Family Child Care Regulation

Definition:	1–5 = family child care, including provider's children under 5 years
Type of regulation:	License
Number of inspections per year:	4
Training required:	None
Criminal record check?	No
Child abuse record check?	No

Oregon

State Regulatory Agency

Department of Human Resources
Children's Services Division
198 Commercial Street, SE
Salem, OR 97310
(503) 378-3178

Statewide Resource and Referral Network

Oregon Child Care Resource and Referral Network
325 Thirteenth Street, NE, Suite 206
Salem, OR 97301
(503) 585-6232

Features of Child Care Center Regulation

Child:staff ratios:	1-year-olds, 4:1
	3-year-olds, 10:1
	5-year-olds, 15:1
Number of inspections per year:	1
Training required:	Preservice and first-aid training
Criminal record check?	Yes
Child abuse record check?	Yes

Features of Family Child Care Regulation

Definition:	1–6 = family child care, maximum of 2 under 2 years, including provider's children under 6 years; 7–12 = group home, maximum of 4 under 30 months
Type of regulation:	Voluntary license for family child care; license for group home
Number of inspections per year:	0
Training required:	None
Criminal record check?	Yes
Child abuse record check?	Yes

Pennsylvania

State Regulatory Agency

Department of Public Welfare
Central Region Day Care Services
P.O. Box 2675
Lanco Lodge Building 25
Harrison, PA 17105
(717) 772-4400

Statewide Resource and Referral Network*

Child Care Choices
125 South Ninth Street, Suite 603
Philadelphia, PA 19107
(215) 592-7644

Child Care Consultants, Inc.
376 East Market Street
York, PA 17403
(717) 854-CARE

Child Placement Network, Inc.
2720 Potshop Road
Norristown, PA 19403
(215) 584-0960

Community Services for Children, Inc.
431 East Locust Street
Bethlehem, PA 18018
(215) TOT-INFO

Delaware Valley Child Care Resource and Referral Center
840 West Main Street, 3rd Floor
Lansdale, PA 19446
(800) VIP-KIDS

International Institute of Erie
P.O. Box 486
Erie, PA 16512
(814) 452-3935

Probe
3400 Trindle Road
Camp Hill, PA 17011
(717) 737-2584

United Way's Child Care Network
200 Ross Street, Suite 600
Pittsburgh, PA 15219
(412) 392-3131

Features of Child Care Center Regulation

Child:staff ratios:	1-year-olds, 5:1
	3-year-olds, 10:1
	5-year-olds, 10:1
Number of inspections per year:	1
Training required:	Preservice and first-aid training
Criminal record check?	Yes
Child abuse record check?	Yes

Features of Family Child Care Regulation

Definition:	4–6 = family child care, maximum of 4 under 2 years, including provider's children under 6 years; 7–11 = group home, maximum of 8 under 2 years
Type of regulation:	Registration for family child care; license for group home
Number of inspections per year:	20% sample
Training required:	Unspecified ongoing training
Criminal record check?	Yes
Child abuse record check?	Yes

Rhode Island

State Regulatory Agency

Department of Children and Their Families
610 Mount Pleasant Avenue, Building 10
Providence, RI 02908
(401) 457-4708

Statewide Resource and Referral Network

Options for Working Parents
30 Exchange Terrace
Providence, RI 02903
(401) 272-7510

Features of Child Care Center Regulation

Child:staff ratios:	1-year-olds, 6:1
	3-year-olds, 15:1
	5-year-olds, 25:1
Number of inspections per year:	1
Training required:	Preservice and first-aid training
Criminal record check?	Yes
Child abuse record check?	No

Features of Family Child Care Regulation

Definition:	4–6 = family child care, maximum of 2 under 2 years, including provider's children under 12 years; 9–12 = group home, maximum of 4 under 2 years
Type of regulation:	License
Number of inspections per year:	1 per 2 years
Training required:	None
Criminal record check?	Yes
Child abuse record check?	No

South Carolina

State Regulatory Agency

Department of Social Services
Day Care Licensing Division
P.O. Box 1520
Columbia, SC 29202
(803) 734-5740

Statewide Resource and Referral Network

South Carolina Child Care Resource and Referral Network
2129 Santee Avenue
Columbia, SC 29205
(803) 254-9263

Features of Child Care Center Regulation

Child:staff ratios: 1-year-olds, 8:1
                                          3-year-olds, 15:1
                                          5-year-olds, 25:1
Number of inspections per year: Varies
Training required: Preservice and health training
Criminal record check?   Yes
Child abuse record check?   Yes

Features of Family Child Care Regulation

Definition: 1–6 = family child care, including
                                          provider's children under 12 years;
                                          7–12 = group home, maximum of 3
                                          under 2 years
Type of regulation: License for subsidized family child
                                          care only
Number of inspections per year: 0
Training required: None
Criminal record check?   No
Child abuse record check?   No

South Dakota

State Regulatory Agency

Department of Social Services
Child Protection Services
700 Governor's Drive
Pierre, SD 57501
(605) 773-3227

Statewide Resource and Referral Network*

Child Development and Family Relations
South Dakota State University
Box 2218
Brookings, SD 57007
(605) 688-5730

Positive Parent Network
P.O. Box 2792
Rapid City, SD 57709
(605) 348-9276

Features of Child Care Center Regulation

Child:staff ratios:	1-year-olds, 5:1
	3-year-olds, 10:1
	5-year-olds, 10:1
Number of inspections per year:	1–12
Training required:	Preservice and health training
Criminal record check?	No
Child abuse record check?	Yes

Features of Family Child Care Regulation

Definition:	1–12 = family child care, maximum of 5 under 3 years, including provider's preschoolers; 13–20 = group home, maximum of 10 under 3 years
Type of regulation:	Registration for subsidized family child care; license for group home
Number of inspections per year:	1–12
Training required:	None
Criminal record check?	No
Child abuse record check?	Yes

Tennessee

State Regulatory Agency

Department of Human Services
Day Care Licensing Division
900 Second Avenue North
Nashville, TN 37201-1030
(615) 244-9706

Statewide Resource and Referral Network

Tennessee Child Care Resource and Referral Services
TN DHS/Day Care Services
400 Deaderick Street
Nashville, TN 37248-9600
(615) 741-0290

Features of Child Care Center Regulation

Child:staff ratios:	1-year-olds, 5:1/7:1
	3-year-olds, 10:1
	5-year-olds, 20:1
Number of inspections per year:	2
Training required:	First-aid training
Criminal record check?	No
Child abuse record check?	No

Features of Family Child Care Regulation

Definition:	5–7 = family child care, maximum of 4 under 2 years, not including provider's children; 8–12 = group home, maximum of 9 under 3 years
Type of regulation:	License
Number of inspections per year:	2
Training required:	2 hours of training each year
Criminal record check?	No
Child abuse record check?	No

Texas

State Regulatory Agency

Department of Human Services
Day Care Licensing Division
P.O. Box 149030
Austin, TX 78769
(512) 450-3261

Statewide Resource and Referral Network

Texas Association of Child Care Resource and Referral Agencies
4029 Capital of Texas Highway South, Suite 102
Austin, TX 78704
(512) 440-8555

Features of Child Care Center Regulation

Child:staff ratios:	1-year-olds, 5:1/12:2; 3-year-olds, 10:1; 5-year-olds, 20:1
Number of inspections per year:	2
Training required:	Preservice
Criminal record check?	Yes
Child abuse record check?	Yes

Features of Family Child Care Regulation

Definition:	4–6 = family child care, maximum of 4 under 18 months, not including provider's children; 7–12 = group home, maximum of 10 under 18 months if all children are under 18 months
Type of regulation:	Registration for family child care; license for group home
Number of inspections per year:	0
Training required:	None
Criminal record check?	Yes
Child abuse record check?	Yes

Utah

State Regulatory Agency

Division of Human Services
Office of Licensing
120 North 200 West
Salt Lake City, UT 84145-0500
(801) 538-4100

Statewide Resource and Referral Network*

Children First
5215 Greenpine Drive
Murray, UT 84123
(801) 268-9492

Children's Service Society
576 East South Temple
Salt Lake City, UT 84102
(801) 537-1044

Features of Child Care Center Regulation

Child:staff ratios:	1-year-olds, 4:1
	3-year-olds, 15:1
	5-year-olds, 20:1
Number of inspections per year:	3
Training required:	Preservice
Criminal record check?	No
Child abuse record check?	Yes

Features of Family Child Care Regulation

Definition:	3–6 = family child care, maximum of 2 under 2 years, including provider's children under 6 years; 7–12 = group home, maximum of 4 under 2 years
Type of regulation:	License
Number of inspections per year:	1 per 2 years
Training required:	2 hours of prelicensing training
Criminal record check?	No
Child abuse record check?	No

Vermont

State Regulatory Agency

Department of Social Services
Day Care Licensing and Regulations Division
103 South Main Street
Waterbury, VT 05676

Statewide Resource and Referral Network

Vermont Association of Child Care Resource and Referral Agencies
Early Childhood Programs
Vermont College
Montpelier, VT 05602
(802) 828-8675

Features of Child Care Center Regulation

Child:staff ratios:	1-year-olds, 4:1
	3-year-olds, 10:1
	5-year-olds, 10:1
Number of inspections per year:	2
Training required:	Preservice and first-aid training
Criminal record check?	No
Child abuse record check?	Yes

Features of Family Child Care Regulation

Definition:	3–6 = family child care, maximum of 2 under 2 years, not including provider's children
Type of regulation:	Registration
Number of inspections per year:	2
Training required:	6 hours per year
Criminal record check?	No
Child abuse record check?	Yes (licensed homes only)

Virginia

State Regulatory Agency

Department of Social Services
8007 Discovery Drive
Blair Building
Richmond, VA 23229-8699
(804) 662-9025

Statewide Resource and Referral Network

Virginia Child Care Resource and Referral Network
3701 Pender Drive
Fairfax, VA 22030
(703) 218-3730

Features of Child Care Center Regulation

Child:staff ratios:	1-year-olds, 4:1
	3-year-olds, 10:1
	5-year-olds, 12:1
Number of inspections per year:	2
Training required:	Preservice and health training
Criminal record check?	Yes
Child abuse record check?	No

Features of Family Child Care Regulation

Definition:	4–9 = family child care, maximum of 4 infants, including provider's children
Type of regulation:	License
Number of inspections per year:	2
Training required:	None
Criminal record check?	Yes
Child abuse record check?	No

Washington

State Regulatory Agency

Department of Social and Health Services
State Office Building 2
Mail Stop OB-41
Olympia, WA 98504
(206) 586-2688

Statewide Resource and Referral Network

Washington State Child Care Resource and Referral Network
P.O. Box 1241
Tacoma, WA 98401
(206) 383-1735

Features of Child Care Center Regulation

Child:staff ratios:	1-year-olds, 7:1
	3-year-olds, 10:1
	5-year-olds, 10:1
Number of inspections per year:	2
Training required:	Preservice and first-aid training
Criminal record check?	Yes
Child abuse record check?	Yes

Features of Family Child Care Regulation

Definition:	1–10 = family child care, maximum of 2 under 2 years, including provider's children under 12 years; 7–12 = group home, maximum of 4 under 2 years
Type of regulation:	License
Number of inspections per year:	0
Training required:	None
Criminal record check?	Yes
Child abuse record check?	Yes

West Virginia

State Regulatory Agency

Department of Health and Human Services
State Capitol Building 6, Room 850
Charleston, WV 25305
(304) 348-7980

Statewide Resource and Referral Network

Central Child Care of West Virginia, Inc.
1205 Quarrier Street
Charleston, WV 25361
(304) 340-3667

Features of Child Care Center Regulation

Child:staff ratios:	1-year-olds, 4:1
	3-year-olds, 10:1
	5-year-olds, 15:1
Number of inspections per year:	1
Training required:	Preservice and health training
Criminal record check?	Yes
Child abuse record check?	Yes

Features of Family Child Care Regulation

Definition:	1–6 = family child care, not including provider's children
Type of regulation:	Voluntary registration
Number of inspections per year:	1
Training required:	None
Criminal record check?	Yes
Child abuse record check?	Yes

Wisconsin

State Regulatory Agency

Department of Health and Social Services
Day Care Licensing
3601 Memorial Drive
Madison, WI 53704
(608) 249-0441

Statewide Resource and Referral Network

Wisconsin Child Care Improvement Project
315 West 5th
P.O. Box 369
Hayward, WI 54843
(715) 634-3905

Features of Child Care Center Regulation

Child:staff ratios:	1-year-olds, 4:1
	3-year-olds, 10:1
	5-year-olds, 17:1
Number of inspections per year:	Varies
Training required:	Preservice and health training
Criminal record check?	No
Child abuse record check?	No

Features of Family Child Care Regulation

Definition:	4–8 = family child care, maximum of 3 under 1 year, including provider's children under 7 years
Type of regulation:	License
Number of inspections per year:	Varies
Training required:	40 hours of training in early childhood education in first six months
Criminal record check?	No
Child abuse record check?	No

Wyoming

State Regulatory Agency

Division of Social Services
Family Services Unit
Hathaway Building, 3rd Floor
Cheyenne, WY 82002
(307) 777-7561

Statewide Resource and Referral Network

Day Care Resource and Referral Service
625 South Beverly
Casper, WY 82609
(307) 472-5535

Features of Child Care Center Regulation

Child:staff ratios:	1-year-olds, 5:1
	3-year-olds, 10:1
	5-year-olds, 20:1
Number of inspections per year:	1
Training required:	First-aid training
Criminal record check?	No
Child abuse record check?	No

Features of Family Child Care Regulation

Definition:	3–6 = family child care, maximum of 2 under 2 years, including provider's preschoolers; 7–11 = group home
Type of regulation:	Registration for family child care; license for group home
Number of inspections per year:	Varies
Training required:	None
Criminal record check?	No
Child abuse record check?	No

Sources

Berzin, Judith. *The Complete Guide to Choosing Child Care*. New York: Random House, 1990.

Child Care Action Campaign. *Child Care Fact Sheet*. New York: 1990.

Children's Defense Fund. *Who Knows How Safe?* Washington, DC: 1990.

Children's Defense Fund. *The State of America's Children*. Washington, DC: 1991.

Gnezda, M. Therese, and Shelley L. Smith. *Child Care and Early Childhood Education Policy: A Legislator's Guide*. Washington, DC: National Conference of State Legislators, 1989.

Morgan, Gwen. *The National State of Child Care Regulation, 1989* . Washington, DC: National Association for the Education of Young Children, 1991.

Glossary

Augustus F. Hawkins Human Services Reauthorization Act of 1990 Legislation that reauthorized the State Dependent Care Development Grants, Head Start funding, and Child Development Associate Scholarship Assistance Act.

Child Care and Development Block Grant Child care provision of the Omnibus Budget Reconciliation Act of 1990, which provides funds for child care services to low-income working families under a sliding fee scale established by each state. Funds are also to be used for activities to improve the availability and quality of child care.

child care center A public or private facility designated primarily for the care of children. Types of child care centers can include preschools, nursery schools, Head Start programs, and full-day programs.

child care provider Person whose professional career choice is caring for children.

consortium center A child care center formed by a collaborating group of employers who share the costs and benefits of establishing it.

dependent care assistance program (DCAP) A tax-exempt employee fringe benefit in which an employer provides a child/elder care "allowance." Since the DCAP is not considered part of the employee's salary, the employee does not owe federal income or social security taxes on the amount of assistance.

Dependent Care Tax Credit Federal tax credit that may be applied against the costs of care for children under the age of 15, as well as for a dependent of any age, including a spouse who is physically or mentally incapable of caring for him- or herself. The amount of the credit is determined by the adjusted gross income shown on the individual's federal income tax return.

developmentally appropriate practice (DAP) Educational programs that are sensitive to the age groups of the children they serve and to the individual needs of each child in the group.

Earned Income Tax Credit (EITC) A refundable tax credit available to low-income working families with a child under 19.

family child care (also family day care) Child care offered in the private home of a provider.

family child care network A group of family child care providers who have been recruited by a company to provide care for employees' children.

Federal Interagency Day Care Requirements (FIDCR) Minimum quality standards established for federally sponsored child care programs; implementation of standards was permanently suspended in 1981.

flexplace An option for employees to complete all or part of their employment responsibilities at home.

flextime Employees choose the time they arrive at work and the time they leave, as long as they accumulate the required number of hours per day or week.

group child care homes Child care offered in the private home of a provider, with the assistance of another caregiver.

Head Start Federally funded compensatory early education programs for environmentally and economically disadvantaged children.

in-home child care Child care provided in the child's home, often by a nanny or au pair.

job sharing Two compatible workers share the responsibilities and wages of one full-time job.

latchkey children School-age children who care for themselves before and/or after school.

maternity leave paid or unpaid leave for new mothers to recover from childbirth.

Omnibus Budget Reconciliation Act of 1990 Legislation in which was included the Child Care and Development Block Grant, a new child care services entitlement under the Family Support Act, an expansion of the Earned Income Tax Credit, and new and expanded tax credits designed to assist low-income families.

on-site child care A child care facility established at an employee's workplace or at a site conveniently located near the workplace.

parental leave Paid or unpaid leave during which parents attend to family matters such as birth or adoption of child, elder care responsibilities, or serious illness.

Pregnancy Disability Act of 1978 Ensures that pregnant women must receive the same leave time and benefits as other disabled workers.

reduced workweek Employees are allowed to reduce their work time and pay by 5–50 percent for a specified period to meet family needs.

resource and referral service Community-based agency or office that informs parents about available forms of child care, provides technical assistance to child care providers, and consults with employers on child care-related issues.

salary redirection Special account established by employer using a tax exempt portion of a participating employee's salary from which that employee can pay child care expenses; federal government limit is $5,000 per year.

school-age child care (also before- and after-school child care) Child care provided for children between the ages of 5 and 13, before and after school and during school vacations and holidays.

shared care Child care situation in which several families employ one provider to care for all of their children in one of their homes.

sick child care programs Child care for children who are mildly ill or recovering from health problems; can be provided in a "sick bay" in a child care center or family child care home, a special hospital ward, or the child's home by visiting nurse–type services.

Title IV of the Social Security Act Authorized a new entitlement for child care so that child care funds are available on a sliding-scale basis to any family the state determines is not receiving Aid to Families with Dependent Children, needs child care in order to work, and is at risk of becoming dependent on AFDC.

vendor program   Child care benefit in which employer reserves or purchases spaces in existing child care programs for employee's use.

voucher system   Employer-financed system of payment to child care provider of parent's choice.

Index